Retire Ready

Retire Ready

Minding Your Money In Your 60s & Beyond

Stoddart

Published in 1998 by Stoddart Publishing Co. Limited
34 Lesmill Road, Toronto, Canada M3B 2T6
Toll-free tel. for Ontario & Quebec: 1-800-387-0141
Toll-free tel. for all other provinces & territories: 1-800-287-0172
Fax: (416) 445-5967   Email: customer.service@ccmailgw.genpub.com

Stoddart Books are available for bulk purchase for sales promotions, premiums, fundraising, and seminars. For details, contact the Special Sales Department at the above address.

Produced for Investors Group by Alpha Media™
151 Bloor St. W., Suite 890, Toronto, Canada M5S 1S4

02 01 00 99 98 1 2 3 4 5

Canadian Cataloguing in Publication Data

Main entry under title:

Retire ready: minding your money in your 60s & beyond

(The Investors Group series)
ISBN 0-7737-5949-2

1. Retirees — Canada — Finance, Personal.   2. Retirement income — Canada — Planning.   I. Investors Group.   II. Series

HG179.R47 1998   332.024'0696   C97-932567-6

JACKET AND TEXT DESIGN: Adele Webster/ArtPlus Limited
COVER ILLUSTRATION: Riccardo Stampatori
PAGE MAKE-UP: Valerie Bateman/ArtPlus Limited

Printed and bound in Canada

About Investors Group

Investors Group is a Canadian leader in providing personal financial services through financial planning, a unique family of mutual funds, and a comprehensive range of other investment products and services including retirement savings plans, insurance, mortgages, and GICs.

The Investors Group story began in 1940, and we have grown to serve close to one million clients from coast to coast through a dedicated and professional sales force. At the heart of our efforts is a simple, long-term strategy — to work closely with clients to understand their current circumstances and investment preferences and help them achieve their long-term personal and financial goals.

Investors Group is a member of the Power Financial Corporation group of companies.

Acknowledgments

This book was the result of a collaboration among people at three companies. Susan Yates and Arnold Gosewich at Alpha Media initiated and co-ordinated the project. At Investors Group, a large and dedicated team of Chartered Financial Planners, accountants, lawyers, and investment specialists provided tax and financial planning information, as well as general direction on appropriate strategies for consumers in each life stage. At Colborne Communications Centre, Greg Ioannou, Sasha Chapman, and Nancy Carr co-ordinated the writing, editing, and indexing.

About This Book

Retire Ready is a book for retirees who want to take control of their financial lives by learning the principles of investing and money management. No matter how long you've been retired, the book will equip you to think more clearly and usefully about your own situation and will arm you with questions you can ask to help you achieve your dreams. This book is not written as a "do it yourself" guide. In fact, many of the subjects discussed involve complex legal, financial, and tax issues that we have tried to simplify to make them more approachable.

Because the details of each life are different, it would be impossible to cover all of life's possibilities in one place. Readers are urged to seek professional advice on their personal circumstances.

About This Series

Retire Ready is the third book in a four-part series designed to help different groups of people take control of their financial lives. The other three books are

Starting Out, for beginning investors;

Prime Time, for intermediate investors, and especially those who are focused on retirement planning; and

Small Business, a book designed to address the special financial needs of the small business owner.

Contents

CHAPTER 1

Lifestyle Choices and Your Retirement

A Secure and Comfortable Retirement

Comfort. Security. Freedom from worry that you will outlive your savings. That's what financial planning is all about. No matter who you are, or how old you are, you have a lifestyle that you want to improve or at least maintain. And that way of life has a price tag. Maybe you want to buy a home in the sunbelt to spend your retirement playing golf or fishing. Perhaps you want to travel. Or maybe you just want to find out where all your money goes. Whatever your lifestyle or your goals, you can make your money go further during your retirement by managing it better.

The Big Secret

Personal finance is not really a cold-blooded, penny-pinching exercise in dollar signs and decimal points. In fact, it's a warm and human activity, because it's all about reaching your dreams. Managing your money allows you to get more for every dollar — and that means you can say yes to yourself more often and more generously. Yes to you, to your goals, and to the life you want to live. The fact that you're reading this book shows that you want to make the best possible life for yourself, and this is the starting point. Everyone deserves personal and family financial independence, and has the ability to achieve it. Add common sense, awareness of your key goals, and a willingness to strengthen some money-preserving habits, and you're on your way.

Good and Not-So-Good Times

WHAT EXACTLY IS FINANCIAL PLANNING ANYWAY?

The keys to financial planning:

- planning your estate to protect your family against loss of income
- minimizing tax
- keeping track of your income and expenses
- planning your income stream
- preparing for unexpected financial obligations
- being able to earn good returns from your investments, with acceptable risk

Financial planning essentially means paying attention to the money you have today and planning ahead for your future.

You have the ability to determine your future. This would be good news, even at the best of times. Since we all go through good times and bad times, it's really good news.

Everything tells us that we're going to have to depend on ourselves more and on others less. The government safety net has been shrinking. In general, it's harder to qualify for benefits and the benefits are smaller. You not only have to rely on your own financial resources more, you'll probably have to do it for a longer time because Canadians are living longer. So financial planning is for you. Take charge of your money and it will cushion your retirement. It will let you enjoy these years by making the most of what you have and making it last.

What Do You Want to Do Now?

Remember those dreams you had about everything you were going to do in retirement? Well, now is the time you've been waiting for. But first, make some informed choices about your new lifestyle and learn about the financial impact that these changes will have. Retirement can be the perfect time to travel, to simply relax and putter around the house, or even to start another career. Whatever your choice, make it part of your financial plans.

FIVE STEPS TOWARD A SECURE, COMFORTABLE RETIREMENT

If you have just retired, these five steps will help ensure that you have a financially independent retirement:

1. Plan carefully to minimize your taxes:
   • Convert your RRSP to a RRIF by age 69.
   • Use all tax deductions and credits available to you.
2. Protect yourself:
   • Make sure your will is current and have a power of attorney drawn up.
   • Match your insurance coverage to your needs and goals.
   • Make sure your family will be financially secure if you or your spouse dies or becomes infirm.
3. Develop an investment strategy:
   • Understand the risks of investment and decide how much risk is appropriate for you.
   • Have your money divided up for use in short-, medium-, and long-term situations.
4. Plan your long-term goals:
   • Know where you want to be in 10 years (i.e., which large lump-sum purchases you'd like to make, such as a new car, a dream trip, or a vacation property), and save for those goals.
5. Manage your debts and expenses:
   • Pay off loans.
   • Develop some good spending habits.
   • Stay on top of debt and pay off your highest-cost debt first.

Dreams and reality are often polar opposites, but they don't have to be. If you set reasonable goals for your retirement lifestyle and use all of your financial savvy to meet them, your dreams will be within reach.

GOING IT ALONE

You always knew that one of you could be left living without the other, but it still comes as a terrible shock: having your spouse suffer a disabling illness or die is traumatic. It's a difficult time emotionally, and you may feel that worrying about money just isn't important, but the loss of a spouse can wreak havoc on your finances, which can make getting back to life more difficult. Getting through it is less painful if you have the support of family and friends, as well as a good financial plan that will take care of you now and later. You may have many years ahead of you, and even though it seems hard to believe after the loss of your partner, those years can still be full of happiness. But it is essential that you have adequate retirement income. When the grief is less, there will still be a future to look to, and going it alone with a strong financial outlook will make you stronger in spite of your loss. Your loved one wouldn't have wanted it any other way.

Taking Charge of Your Financial Life

Your financial plan will be as individual as your thumbprint because it has to fit your goals, your circumstances, and your lifestyle. But the basic components are common to all successful financial approaches, and they are reassuringly simple. The key is to identify your major lifestyle goals, set up financial goals to match, and then work out financial strategies that will get you there. So start with information and then apply it.

SOME TIPS FOR GETTING ORGANIZED

Even if organization isn't your strong suit, you will find it easy when you follow these simple steps:

1) Keep track of the cheques you write, automatic payment deductions and debits from your ATM card.
2) Save all relevant documents, such as credit card receipts, debit card slips, investment reports, and income stubs.
3) Set up a filing system. You'll gain immense satisfaction when you need some piece of paper and can put your finger on it instantly. Here's how to set up a filing system.

Buy a two-drawer metal filing cabinet. An accordion folder will do to start. Use a folder (or your safety deposit box, for valuable documents) for each of the following categories.

Statements from financial institutions (separate folder for each institution).

Credit Card(s) The receipts and statements for each in a separate folder.

Investment Folders For such things as RRSPs, RRIFs, annuities, and mutual funds

Home Several folders for documents pertaining to purchase and mortgage (or rent receipts and rental agreement), property tax, repairs, and improvements

Automobile Folders for financing, bill of sale, repairs

Income Tax and Tax-Deductible Items One folder for your previous year's tax form and notice of assessment, and one for all the tax slips and receipts for the current tax year

Insurance A folder for each kind of insurance (e.g., auto, home, life, disability)

Personal Papers Your birth certificate, social insurance card, marriage or divorce papers, passport, will, and other important papers

Salary Paycheque stubs and any other job-related documents

Self-Employment Records If you're self-employed, keep a record of invoices rendered. You'll likely need folders for each type of deductible expense.

Warranties, Receipts, Instruction Manuals Keep these for all purchases, both large and small. These may not be part of your financial plan, but they sure make life easier when kept in one place.

- Identify the most important elements of the lifestyle you want in retirement.
- Work out how much money you'll need to maintain the lifestyle you want. Be prepared to make some adjustments, if necessary.
- Assess your current financial situation: income, fixed expenses, discretionary spending, assets, and liabilities. Project it over the period of time you expect to enjoy retirement.
- Calculate whether you'll be able to make your finances last your lifetime. You might have to make some changes now, for future benefit. This can be a difficult task, so contact a professional financial advisor for help. Progressive advisors have access to computer programs that can show you projections on your income and expenses for the length of your retirement.

The Big Three Principles

For the greatest possible financial strength throughout your life, follow these three simple principles:

- Choose your income stream carefully, with emphasis on tax considerations.
- Minimize your taxes.
- Pay off high-cost, non-deductible debts and enter new debt wisely.

How Long Will You Be Retired?

You hope for a good long time, and in the best of health. But how can you know? The simple answer is, you can't. It's a delicate question, but it needs examining in order for you to make your decisions wisely. Canadian men who are in their mid-sixties can expect to live, on average, into their early eighties. Women in the same age group can expect to live to their late eighties.

A couple who retires together around the age of 65 will find that the odds are fairly good that one of them will live into their nineties, so retirement planning must encompass the surviving spouse's needs. Unfortunately, planning for uncertainty is not a good position to bargain from, and the best option is to be optimistic. This is one of the areas of your life in which optimism can equal good planning. You or your spouse might not live to 90, but if you think and act as though you will, you'll be better prepared. Even if your resources won't realistically stretch that far, you can still plan ahead with what you have, with a mind to budgeting for now as well as later.

They may not be glamorous, but these principles are incredibly powerful. The trick is to work out how to stay faithful to them as you make your way through the surprises and changes of life. That's where you'll need to devise strategies and systems, make tradeoffs, and juggle priorities. But if you keep focused on the three principles, many other choices become clearer. The principles will be discussed in more detail later in the book.

THE BASIC PHILOSOPHY

At least once a year, assess your financial situation. Establish a realistic and comfortable plan to maintain your lifestyle. You don't need to do everything yourself. Use a financial advisor the same way you would use a physician — take advantage of their expertise to ensure your financial health.

WHAT'S YOUR FINANCIAL HEALTH?

GOOD SIGNS

- You've established your lifestyle priorities, with financial goals to match.
- You know how much you can afford to spend each month, and you stick to it pretty faithfully.
- You've set aside money for emergencies, and you have set up plans in case you become ill or die.
- You're keeping track of your investments and looking for ways to maximize their growth, without incurring too much risk.
- You make tax time less painful by ensuring that you are getting all the deductions and credits coming to you.
- You feel good about money because you are in control.
- You sleep well at night and you never feel stressed about your family finances.
- You and your spouse both know what provisions you have made for each other should one of you die.
- You have a current will and power of attorney.

BAD SIGNS

- You're spending what you have, without thinking about how long it will last.
- You don't balance your accounts. In fact, you don't even know how much is in your accounts.
- You have no plan to deal with the unexpected, since you don't expect any major disasters to happen.
- You worry about a market crash and find yourself overreacting to every movement in the market.
- You can't really afford your yearly tax bill but you just pay what the government asks for, without looking at how you can reduce that amount.
- You're helping out your kids or grandchildren without thinking of your own financial future.
- You worry that you may have to return to work to make ends meet.
- You don't know what provisions your spouse has made for you, but you're assuming you'll be looked after.
- You haven't updated your will in years and don't have a power of attorney.

NO MORE YO-YO FINANCIAL PLANNING!

• Kick the starvation-diet approach, and start enjoying yourself. Starvation, financial or otherwise, doesn't work. A common-sense approach does.

• Make financial awareness part of your daily lifestyle.

• Have a balanced financial diet: preserve your assets, monitor results. Adjust as appropriate.

• Remember: every healthy diet includes treats. Just don't overdo it.

• Think about your long-term financial health, and build in activities now that will safeguard you in years to come.

• Keep it simple.

• Don't be afraid to ask! You wouldn't do your own surgery or defend yourself in court.

• Professional advisors working with a reputable firm can help you plan and achieve your goals.

You and the Experts

Many experts are out there to advise you, explain things to you, and provide you with products and services. They range from stockbrokers to financial advisors, accountants, portfolio managers, insurance agents, and lawyers. If you already rely on a financial expert, are you happy with the service you are getting? Remember, experts want your business, so it pays to shop around to find out which one will best suit your needs. Choose your financial advisor the same way you would pick your doctor or dentist. Friends' recommendations can help, but also check credentials and go with your instincts. You need to find someone you feel comfortable with and trust.

No matter how carefully you pick and how confident you are in your "normal" life, you may feel tongue-tied when you actually sit down with the financial expert. Here's how to get the best from the meeting:

- Do your homework. Fill in any forms you've been given in advance, bring any papers you have been asked to supply, and write out the questions you want answered during the meeting. Be prepared to provide details of all your family finances. It may make you uncomfortable at first but advisors need all the information to do the best job for you.

- Expect the financial planner to have done his or her homework as well. Is the person ready for the meeting? Familiar with your file and background material? Equipped with everything needed to carry out the day's agenda?

- Listen carefully. Ask questions whenever you want more information, or when you don't understand what your advisor is saying. Don't be intimidated! It's not up to you to guess, it's up to the expert to be clear. Professionals will welcome your questions because they want you to understand. Be suspicious of those who brush you off.

- Take notes. Things that seem clear at the time may blur in your memory later.

- Cover every topic that was on your list, but don't waste time. Check to see if you are being charged by the hour, but even if the session is free or flat rate, it's courteous to stay focused.

- Do any necessary follow-up, and make sure that the expert does, too.

- Above all, remember that decisions are ultimately up to you. It's your life and your money. Experts can advise and help, but you are in charge. This is a responsibility, as well as a right.

Summary

Just because you are retired doesn't mean that you don't still need to set financial goals for yourself. To get where you want to go, you first have to know where you are going. So before you do anything, ask yourself a few questions that will keep the rest of your financial planning on track:

- How can I manage my retirement income stream?
- How can I prioritize my needs and wants for my retirement?
- How can I match my healthy cash management habits with my lifestyle and financial goals?
- Are my investments keeping up?
- Do I need to reduce my spending?
- Do I know enough about taxes, investments, and strategies to do this without a professional advisor?

The answer to many of these questions is just to be aware of your financial situation — even if you have never paid much attention to your finances, it's not too late to start! Don't forget to assess your financial situation at least once a year during your retirement.

ONE MORE TIME: THE BIG THREE PRINCIPLES

1. **Choose your income stream carefully, with emphasis on tax considerations.**

2. **Minimize your taxes.**

3. **Pay off high-cost, non-deductible debts and enter new debt wisely.**

CHAPTER 2

Making Plans

Whether or not you've thought about it, you probably have a conscious (or unconscious) financial plan. But how do you begin to give that plan some direction? Or reassess it when your circumstances change?

New Possibilities, New Spending

Being retired doesn't mean your previous life as a consumer ends and you'll now spend your time sitting in an easy chair, living frugally so that you can pass on your money to your children. In fact, being retired can mean you spend even more. And why not? You've worked hard, and now you have the chance to reap the benefits. Your choice of purchases has likely changed quite a bit over the years, but the basics of buying never change: buy only what's important and affordable to you. If you have to enter into debt, do so sensibly, by choosing the most appropriate financing and paying it off.

Sally and Laszlo

Sally, 58, and her husband Laszlo, 62, have been looking forward to this time in their lives for years. Sally is going to close down the importing business she started (Italian leather goods) when her two children moved out 10 years ago. Laszlo is a sales manager in a pharmaceuticals company, but his job has always kept him on the road. He has decided to take retirement three years early because he wants to spend more time with Sally in their own home. In fact, his first big project for retirement is to build a big bay window in their living room and a deck just outside. Sally and Laszlo own their home, they both have RRSPs, and Laszlo has almost a full company pension plan, but the couple has never done much investing other than that and they don't know how much (or how little) government support they will be entitled to. They'd like to learn how to make their money keep growing during their retirement, while still being able to leave some to their grown children and future grandchildren.

Lloyd

Lloyd is a 75-year-old former Olympic swimmer whose wife died eight years ago, just after he retired. After grieving for his wife for a long time, Lloyd recently resolved to make the most of the rest of his life — he got back into shape and decided to spend more time with his children and grandchildren at his lakefront vacation property. He is also thinking about selling his townhouse in the city and getting a condominium on a tropical beach; that way he could live at his vacation property in the summer and on the beach in the winter. Lloyd is pretty well set up with RRIFs and other investments, but he hasn't reassessed his estate since his wife's death and isn't sure if some changes need to be made.

The Future Begins in the Present

Sally, Laszlo, and Lloyd all feel uncertain about their situations. They don't feel fully in control of where they are, or where they are going. You may be feeling exactly the same way. Given the rapid changes taking place, how can anyone predict his or her own financial future?

Although no one can give you the financial-planning equivalent of a crystal ball, there are ways to figure out what your various options are and what's possible for you. The trick is to start by figuring out where you are today.

The Big Picture

This book will take you through a simple, logical series of steps to organize your financial life.

Step 1   Determine your life goals. It is impossible to plan unless you know what you are aiming for.

Step 2   Determine your net worth. That is, find out where you are starting.

Step 3   Figure out how much you'll need in order to finance your life goals.

Step 4   Examine your current sources of income, and look to see what you are spending it on. Using a simple expense diary will make it easy. Keep track of your income and expenses for two months.

Step 5   Prepare a budget that will let you live in comfort today while ensuring you are preserving enough of your capital to meet your goals.

Step 1: Determine Your Life Goals

Only you can identify your life goals and priorities. Do this first: everything else depends on it. Once you know what's most important in your life, you decide on the financial goals and strategies that will let you shape the life you want.

After all, you won't get very far if you don't know where you are going. To come up with a list of goals you will need to have a clear idea of what you want now and later. What do you want to accomplish? How soon would you like these things to happen? Make sure that your goals are realistic. Once you've drawn up a list of goals, try to measure your progress and to reassess your goals once a year.

Here's a list of typical goals:

- protect my spouse financially if I die
- enjoy a warmer climate during the winter, either through trips or buying property
- join a golf or tennis club
- travel (to South America, India, Antarctica, New Jersey, etc.)
- plan for lump-sum purchases, such as a car every 10 years during retirement
- work, consult — or study
- leave an inheritance
- spend time doing volunteer work or donate to charities

SEEING THE WORLD

After spending so many years working or raising a family, with only a few weeks' holiday a year, retirement seems the perfect chance to make up for lost time and to do some travelling. If you've been planning some fabulous trips for years, chances are you've been putting aside some cash to finance them. If you haven't, you may need to adjust some other expenses and do some travel planning.

By all means, enjoy your new freedom and the new worlds that retirement can open up for you. Even if you can't afford a holiday to a different country every year, you might plan a major trip every two or three years, giving yourself time to do research on your chosen destination, and discover some places closer to home in the meantime.

TRAVEL INSURANCE

Along with your camera, travellers' cheques, and tour guide, make sure to take another essential: travel insurance. Maybe you'll never use it, but it will let you enjoy your trip without worrying about the financial consequences of the unexpected.

Your provincial health insurance will cover only a small portion of emergency care costs, should you need medical treatment while in another country. Alberta and Saskatchewan will pay $100 per day for foreign hospital bills, and B.C. will pay only $75. With the astronomical cost of medical care in U.S. hospitals, this amount would barely cover your TV rental fees. Your employer pension fund might provide travel insurance, as may your credit card companies. If you are using credit card coverage, find out whether you have to finance the trip using that credit card to get the free travel insurance. If you have no other coverage, take a look at private travel medical insurance. Most financial institutions offer plans that vary in price and details of coverage. At tax time, you can claim the premiums you pay as a medical expenses tax credit. You'll have to give details of your medical history as part of the approval process and possibly have a checkup before leaving on your trip. Some plans will exclude you if you've had a medical condition within the last 90 days, and other plans won't cover any pre-existing medical condition after you reach a certain age. If you have an unstable medical problem when you leave on your trip, your plan likely will not cover it.

SHOP AROUND!

The Canadian Life and Health Insurance Association will provide you with a free shopping list. For a list of insurers, call 1-800-268-8099, or 416-777-2344 in Toronto.

Consider your life goals, then list them in the first column of the box below in order of priority. In the second column, write in the date by which you'd like to reach these goals. In the third column, list how much money you think you'll need to reach each goal. Some goals, such as buying a new condo, are best represented by a monthly figure. Others, such as paying for a new car, can be represented by a lump sum.

WHAT I WANT	HOW SOON I'D LIKE IT	HOW MUCH I THINK IT WILL COST
1. _____	_____	_____
2. _____	_____	_____
3. _____	_____	_____
4. _____	_____	_____
5. _____	_____	_____
6. _____	_____	_____
7. _____	_____	_____
8. _____	_____	_____
9. _____	_____	_____
10. _____	_____	_____

Step 2: Determine Your Net Worth

What are you worth?
To determine how much you are worth, that is, your net worth, simply subtract your liabilities from your assets. This calculation will clearly show you your real wealth.

Assets
People can have strange ideas of what constitutes an asset, if they confuse them with things that have sentimental, or personal, value. Your favourite comfy slippers are not an asset. So what is?

An asset is something you own that has value in the marketplace. There are two basic kinds of assets:

- personal use assets
- investment assets

Investment assets include cash, stocks, mutual funds, and bonds. We will discuss them in Chapter 8. Here are some common types of personal use assets:

- principal residence, summer residence (could also be an investment)
- sporting equipment
- appliances (this includes your personal, not business, computer, although its rate of depreciation means it won't be an asset for long)
- vehicles
- furniture
- camera equipment
- jewellery

Liabilities

When you purchase assets, it is important to remember the flip side: liabilities. This is the debt you incur to acquire your assets in circumstances when it doesn't make sense to pay cash. Contrary to what your mother and father told you, taking on debt to acquire assets can work in your favour, as long as you do it sensibly.

Common liabilities including the following:

- mortgages
- loans
- credit cards
- unpaid bills

Sample net worth form

If you have a computer, you can use a program to add up your assets and liabilities and figure out your net worth. Most programs are quite affordable and useful. Or you can just use the following sample form and adjust it to fit your situation.

ASSETS

Deposit accounts
Institution

amount

$ _____

$ _____

total $ _____

Life insurance (cash surrender value)
Company

amount

$ _____

$ _____

total $ _____

Pensions and deferred profit-sharing plans

Company

amount

$ _____

$ _____

total $ _____

Non-registered investments
(stocks, funds, GICs, bonds, mortgages held,
business interests, etc.)
Institution

amount

$ _____

$ _____

total $ _____

RRSPs
Institution

amount

$ _____

$ _____

total $ _____

Real estate (home, cottage, other)

amount

$ _____

$ _____

total $ _____

Other assets (equipment, furnishings, jewellery, art)

amount

$ _____

$ _____

total $ _____

Accounts receivable (loans made to
family and friends, tax refunds owing)

amount

$ _____

$ _____

total $ _____

TOTAL ASSETS $ _____

LIABILITIES

Mortgages

Lender   amount owing

_____ $ _____

Loans

1. Lender   amount owing

_____ $ _____

2. Lender   amount owing

_____ $ _____

Accounts payable

(credit cards, taxes, outstanding bills)   _____

                                                                  _____

                                                                  _____

                                                        total $ _____

Other debt (guarantees, personal obligations)   total $ _____

TOTAL LIABILITIES $ _____

NET WORTH

This is the big one. Subtract your total liabilities from your total assets. This is your net worth.

TOTAL ASSETS $ _____

TOTAL LIABILITIES   – $ _____

TOTAL NET WORTH   = $ _____

What Your Assessment Really Means

No matter what your net worth is, going through this exercise gives you invaluable information. Your net worth gives you the whole picture: it tells you if you'll need to make changes in your lifestyle to make your retirement financially secure, and lets you focus on changing the details. Perhaps you've been living on a modest income, worrying about how large a chunk of your income is going to taxes. By switching your asset mix and timing the sale of investments, you may save a lot of money in income taxes. You can then put the money you save toward something more valuable, in terms of both asset building and enjoyment.

Home sweet home

Consider the role your home plays in your asset mix. Do you want to live in it 10 or 20 years from now? Will it be too much to maintain? Even if you still have the energy, the thrill of

---

APPRECIABLE VS DEPRECIABLE

When you are making a major purchase, such as buying a vacation property, a computer, or a car, consider whether the asset is likely to appreciate or depreciate in value. If it is likely to depreciate, how long do you expect to own the asset? Do you expect to resell it? If so, will the difference in value be more than paid for by your use of the asset? Or are you better off renting? If it is likely to appreciate, how long can you expect to wait before you resell it? Would your money be better spent renting the object and putting the difference into a high-yield mutual fund?

painting all that architectural gingerbread may wane. Will you want to pay to have it done? A grand staircase eventually becomes a pain to keep clean, perhaps even to climb. And if you have to sell the place, it may not yield the price you expect. At this point in your life, you may find that you want to sell rather than buy big-ticket items.

Things you should consider before you decide to buy or sell:

- depreciation
- rising maintenance costs
- inflation (good for the value of your house, but a problem if you're living on a fixed retirement income)
- cost-benefit: could you put that money to work in a better investment?
- your present income
- your future needs
- how you will finance a large purchase

Chapter 5 explores the options of choosing where to live in retirement.

Step 3: Figure Out How Much You'll Need in Order to Finance Your Life Goals

It's important to work out what you need to live on during your retirement, and although there's no magic formula, you should take the following three factors into consideration:

1) the number of years you expect to live
2) what you believe you'll need to live on per year
3) the effects of inflation

Step 4: Calculate Your Current Income and Expenses

We suggest keeping an income and expense diary for at least two months. Subtract your expenses from your income. If you're in a good financial situation, this will give you a positive number. If you end up with a negative number, you're eating into your capital. Or perhaps the two numbers are equal — in other words, you're spending everything that comes in, but successfully preserving your assets.

Step 5: Prepare a Budget

When you determined your income and your expenses, you may have discovered that your hard-earned savings aren't exactly going where you want them. Maybe you're spending too much money on rent or your car expenses, or you're simply treating yourself to too many trips to Fort Lauderdale. Now is the time to prepare a budget and actually direct your money where you want it to go. (Please see the sample budget form on the next page.) Look over your budget every so often to see if it is working for you, and change it as needed. Just keep your priorities in mind, and enjoy being in control of your financial life.

The uncommitted income line at the bottom of the budget form is the amount of money you have left over after you've met your predictable day-to-day expenses. You can use this however you want — in effect, it can be added to any expense line in the budget; but you should also consider if it's possible to draw less income from your registered investments and potentially reduce your taxes at the same time.

BUDGET

Net monthly income
Self (pensions, RRIFs, annuities, government programs) $ _____
Spouse (pensions, RRIFs, annuities, government programs) $ _____
Other income (salary, rental income) $ _____

Total net income $ _____

Monthly expenses
Payments on loans and debts $ _____
Mortgage (principal and interest) $ _____
Groceries
– food $ _____
– cleaning supplies $ _____
– other $ _____ $ _____
Clothing $ _____
Shelter
– rent $ _____
– repairs $ _____
– insurance $ _____
– taxes $ _____
– utilities $ _____ $ _____
Transportation
– gas $ _____
– repairs $ _____
– insurance $ _____
– parking $ _____
– other $ _____ $ _____
Insurance premiums (direct medical/dental)
– life $ _____
– disability $ _____
– health $ _____
– other $ _____ $ _____
Recreation/Education
– holidays $ _____
– hobbies $ _____
– clubs $ _____
– subscriptions $ _____ $ _____
Miscellaneous
– donations $ _____
– dues $ _____
– child care/child support $ _____
– alimony $ _____
– other $ _____ $ _____

Total expenses $ _____

Uncommitted income (Total net income less Total expenses) $ _____

Budgeting for the Future

Since the 1950s, inflation rates have averaged 4.5 percent. But, of course, nothing in life is predictable, and inflation rates can soar, as they did when they leapt to 14 percent in the 1980s. To be safe, choose the middle number of 4 percent to figure out your likely expenses from now on.

Now, let's say your expenses come to $30,000 in the first year. Consult the chart below to see what happens to those costs at 4 percent inflation a year.

IMPACT OF INFLATION ON $30,000

	RATE OF INFLATION			
YEAR	**3%**	**4%**	**5%**	**6%**
5	$34,770	$36,510	$38,280	$40,141
10	$40,320	$44,400	$48,870	$53,730
15	$46,740	$54,030	$62,370	$71,910
20	$54,180	$65,730	$79,590	$96,210
30	$72,810	$97,290	$129,660	$172,290

This chart projects how much it will cost to purchase $30,000 worth of goods in the future, based on the assumed rates of inflation.

As you can see, a lifestyle that costs you $30,000 today will cost you $44,400 in your 10th year of retirement, based on 4 percent inflation. Now you see why indexing your income for inflation is key. If you don't, you'll be trying to get by with about 60 percent of what you need to live on in just 10 years.

HABITS THAT HELP

Cutting expenses is the most obvious way of stretching your budget. This list suggests some habits you can develop to make the most of your retirement income. (Many of these ideas are further explained in later chapters.)

✔ Plan ahead for the RRSP conversion deadline: December 31 of the year you turn 69. There are very severe consequences to missing the deadline. See Chapter 4 for details.

✔ Put your retirement savings into a relatively safe but higher income portfolio of investments to increase your return without increasing your risk.

✔ Get your debt under control by paying down higher-cost and non-tax-deductible debt, such as credit card debt. If necessary, pay off that debt with a lower interest loan.

✔ Look at whether you use your credit cards wisely. Pay off the balance each month to avoid paying interest! And beware of those department store cards. The interest rates are astronomical, and most department stores take major credit cards, anyway.

✔ Pay bills promptly to avoid late payment or interest charges.

✔ Become a smart consumer. Research major purchases before buying. Check consumer magazines for repair records and ratings of cars and appliances. Shop around for the best deal and for seniors' discounts.

✔ Make sure you've put some money aside each month to pay your taxes.

✔ Shop around for financial services best suited to retirees. Look for higher rates of return with lower fees or charges.

HABITS THAT HURT

✗ Keeping your money in a low-interest or no-interest savings account just lets inflation eat away at it.

✗ If you're under 69, missing the RRSP deadline because you don't have the cash for a lump sum payment means you pay extra income tax and earn less income — write reminders on your calendar or in your planner. Better yet, contribute throughout the year so that you'll earn income that ends up compounding on a tax-deferred basis. If you are still permanently employed, see if your company has a plan for automatic monthly contributions to an RRSP, which results in reducing the amount of tax deducted from each paycheque.

✗ Signing up for more credit cards than you need just tempts you to spend. Just because a company sends you an application doesn't mean you have to bite.

✗ Missing out on tax-preferred capital gains or dividends by only investing in interest-paying vehicles should be avoided.

✗ Not seeking the advice of an investment professional could cost you.

Following Up

Once you've prepared a financial plan and put it into action you have to follow it up in two ways:

- Monitor your progress. This means doing a net worth assessment at least annually by adding up your assets, subtracting your debts, and seeing how your net worth is changing. The assessment tells you how you're doing and may raise an important warning flag — or give you good cause to pat yourself on the back.
- Reassess your objectives every now and then. Sometimes a big event such as a divorce or a child's marriage makes the need to do so obvious. But you and your situation keep evolving over time, even without big events. Keep in touch with yourself.

Summary

You've outlined your life goals, looked at their financial implications, calculated your net worth, worked out a budget — congratulations! You've taken the first step toward stress-free retirement. The second step, actually putting that plan into action, may be a bit more challenging.

Keep your future in good hands — your own — by making wise financial choices and using your money to your advantage. By educating yourself, you can make your retirement income work for you, and live the life you've always dreamed of.

QUICK RECAP

1. **Determine your life goals.**
2. **Calculate your net worth.**
3. **Prepare a budget to determine your income needs.**

Cashing In on Your Retirement

When you were younger, you probably thought that when you retired, you'd be able to just sit back, watch your pension income roll in, and start those projects you never had time for before. But you've learned, by now, that nothing in life is simple, not even retirement. You may have imagined a life full of free time, but most retirees find they're busier than ever before. They wonder how they ever had time to work!

Your retirement income likely has four main pieces, which create a framework to support you throughout your non-working years. Together, RRSPs and RRIFs, non-registered investments, company pensions, and government support build a secure structure that will withstand inflation and time. By regularly maintaining each part of your retirement income and making wise choices, you'll strengthen your financial support in these later years.

Sources of Retirement Income

RRSPs and RRIFs

Registered Retirement Savings Plans (RRSPs) and Registered Retirement Income Funds (RRIFs) are your best friends when it comes to providing for yourself in retirement. As of age 69, you're required to convert your RRSP to either a RRIF or an annuity. You must "mature" your RRSP no later than the end of the calendar year in which you turn 69, so you must select a retirement income program. This program could be a life annuity (with or without a guaranteed term), a term-certain annuity to age 90, or a RRIF, which has a required minimum payout.

Annuities

Like a RRIF, an annuity is a maturity option for an RRSP, usually exercised by people who have a low risk tolerance or are taking advantage of high interest rates. And when you buy one, you're buying predictability. You hand your money over to an insurance company and then start receiving a monthly cheque based on the interest rate in effect at that time. What's the downside? For one thing, you lose control of your money. For another thing, few annuities offer protection against inflation. Not all annuities have a residual value that would provide money to your estate. If this is important to you, a professional advisor can help you choose from the available product choices.

Who is it for?

Single-life annuities make payments based on one life only; joint-life annuities provide coverage until both you and your spouse die. When considering a joint-life annuity, you can get a quote based on whether the survivor will continue to receive the same amount each month, or a smaller payment.

How long does it last?

Term-certain annuities give you a cheque every month for a specified period of time (e.g., for 10 years). These typically end when you reach 90, if they haven't already. Life annuities, however, keep generating payments as long as you live. Each of these set-ups has a couple of variations. For example, a life annuity would normally stop with your death, but you may choose one with a guarantee period. If you die before that period is up, the remaining payments, or a lump sum for their value, will still be paid to your spouse or beneficiaries. Few people these days opt for a life annuity without a guarantee, even though purchasing the guarantee lowers the monthly payments they receive.

CONSUMER PROTECTION

There is a consumer-protection program for the life-insurance industry, known as CompCorp (Canadian Life and Health Insurance Compensation Corporation), which was launched in 1990. If an insurance company that belongs to CompCorp fails, individual customers are protected, to a certain degree. So when shopping around, ask if the company is a CompCorp member. Here are the limits of CompCorp's protection:

- RRIFs up to $60,000
- Life annuities up to $2,000 a month
- Life insurance up to $200,000

Indexed annuities offer relief from one of annuities' big potential drawbacks: inflation. You'll see a considerable reduction in the monthly payments in the first few years, but if the thought of inflation concerns you, indexed annuity payments can bring you great peace of mind.

Non-Registered Investments

Another source of income is, of course, any investments you hold outside of an RRSP. These might be stocks and bonds, real estate, or other assets that could provide you with an income. See Chapter 8 for more information on different types of investments and Chapter 10 for information on taxation of investment income.

Company Pensions

If you were a member of an employer-sponsored pension plan, you are likely receiving income payments from it. When you meet with your financial advisor, he or she may have questions that you can refer to your former employer for answers.

Government Programs

With all of the cutbacks to government programs, this is probably the smallest part of your retirement income. But by knowing the choices you have, you can at least get the most from each government plan.

Canada Pension Plan/Quebec Pension Plan (CPP/QPP)

The Canada and Quebec Pension Plans cover Canadians who have worked, either as an employee or self-employed. Retirement benefits depend on your record of contributions and when you start taking benefits. You can start as early as 60 or wait as late as 70. For each month you claim before you turn 65, your payment is reduced by 0.5 percent (6 percent a year). For every month you wait after your 65th birthday, your payment increases by 0.5 percent.

You have to take the first step by applying for your benefits. Benefits can start anytime between the ages of 60 and 70, provided that you are "substantially retired." This means that any employment or self-employment income can't exceed the maximum CPP/QPP benefit for those who are 65 years old.

Your benefits will begin one month after you apply. If you are applying as a retiree, the amount is based on your average

TAKE ADVANTAGE OF THE CPP/QPP SPLIT

If your spouse is in a lower tax bracket than you are, and you are receiving CPP/QPP benefits, you can split those benefits with your spouse. That way you won't pay as much tax on the benefits.

indexed pensionable earnings over the length of your working life. Your amount depends on how long you contributed and your income level over your working years. The lowest 15 percent of your qualifying years are excluded from the calculation. So if you contributed for 25 years, the lowest three years of earnings would be dropped. As well, the government makes provision for years taken off work to raise your children and for periods of disability. Even so, CPP/QPP will only pay up to 25 percent of your pre-retirement income. If you are disabled, a surviving spouse, or a dependent child, you may also be able to apply for CPP/QPP. Contact Human Resources Development Canada or the Caisse de dépôt et placement du Québec for more information.

Old age security (OAS)

As soon as you turn 65, you may be eligible for OAS, but you must apply — the payments will not be automatically sent to you. It's a good idea to apply several months before you plan to start using the income from your OAS. The forms are available at post offices and at Income Security Programs offices, part of Human Resources Development Canada or the Caisse de dépôt et placement du Québec.

Eligibility

Your eligibility depends on how long you have lived in Canada. To receive the full benefit, you must have lived in Canada for 10 years prior to your application. You can apply for a partial benefit if you have lived in Canada for at least 10 years since the age of 18. The guidelines apply only to residency, so you'll still be eligible if you have never had paid employment or if you keep working after you turn 65.

Basic OAS payments are taxable, and before you get excited about your new vacation fund (it's not even close to an income), you should know that the money may not be yours to spend. In 1989, the Canadian government introduced a "clawback" to OAS. This clawback was supposed to apply to high-income earners, yet it is affecting the middle class as well. Under the clawback regulations, if your income exceeds a certain limit each year, your OAS payments will be reduced by 15 percent for all net income you earn over this amount. If you have a spouse, and one of you receives more than the limit and the other less, you might be able to rearrange your retirement finances to bring down the higher-income earnings and avoid the clawback. Have the lower-income spouse make withdrawals from their RRSP, if that is an option.

Another possibility for reducing net income is through tax deductions. Don't forget, you can still contribute to RRSPs in your name up until December 31 of the year you turn 69 if you have contribution room. After your 69th birthday, you can keep contributing to your spouse's RRSP until the end of the year he or she turns 69, assuming you have contribution room.

Guaranteed Income Supplement and Spouse's Allowance

If your income is low, you may be entitled to a Guaranteed Income Supplement (GIS) and Spouse's Allowance (SPA). Both benefits are tax free and indexed for inflation. Your benefit depends on a number of factors, such as whether or not your spouse is living and whether your spouse is a pensioner. You'll have to apply every year for these benefits, since they are based on the income you declared in the previous year.

Some provinces supply additional, non-taxable supplements to low-income seniors. Nova Scotia, Ontario, Manitoba, Saskatchewan, Alberta, B.C., the Northwest Territories, and Yukon all have such plans, with varying details. Check the government pages of your phone book for who to call.

Seniors' Benefit

Starting in 2001, a new Seniors' Benefit will take effect for anyone aged 65 or older. The new Seniors' Benefit proposes to replace OAS, GIS, SPA, and the pension and age tax credits. Unlike the OAS, it would be tax-free, but the amount you would be entitled to will be based on a sliding scale measured against your income: the higher the income, the smaller the benefit.

The Empty Nest

There may soon come a time when you will want to downsize the family home. Older retirees find themselves, often enough, strained to maintain substantial homes. When they bought them, they could do most of the work themselves. People caught by the escalating demands (and costs) of aging dwellings often sell, though they would rather have spent their last years in familiar quarters. Others refuse to give up their homes, and become martyrs to them. Some are reluctant to part with valuable property they intend to pass along to their children, though the offspring may find themselves strapped for cash while the family wealth is locked up in real estate.

Once your kids have left home and you have a couple of extra bedrooms, you may want to turn your empty nest into something that can help pay for your retirement. There are a few ways you can do this.

1. Sell the house: move into something smaller and invest the leftover money.
2. Take out a reverse mortgage on your house to supplement your income. A reverse mortgage means you can borrow money using your home as security for the loan. No payments or interest are due until you sell the house or reach the end of the mortgage term.
3. Alter your house so that it will provide income. However, unless the place is already well suited to such a purpose, that option could be less attractive than you might think. Costs could be very high, zoning restrictions may interfere, and in the end you will find that being a landlord or landlady is a part-time job you may not want.

Reverse Mortgages

The reverse mortgage is a loan made out to you against a property you already own, debt-free. If you have property but little income, you can use it to beef up your income and finance anything you want. You don't have to pay the loan in the usual installments; you just continue to own the home and live there (provided it is maintained and insured, and the taxes are paid). When the property is sold, or at the end of a stated term, the loan must be repaid with interest.

The financial institution gives you a line of credit or a lump sum. The total amount of the loan will usually not exceed 35 to 40 percent of the appraised value of the property. If you're so inclined, the loan proceeds can be used to buy an annuity, which in turn provides a regular income. Annuity interest is normally taxed, but in this case the mortgage becomes an investment loan, interest accruing offsets interest paid, and there's no income tax to pay. You can also use a reverse mortgage to pass along some or all of the cash to your children, perhaps to help them buy places of their own, taking the sting out of the encumbrance the property carries when you pass it along to the next generation. You can also tailor the deal so that a minimum portion of the value of the home will go to your estate, even if it's worth less than the amount of the mortgage and its accrued interest.

What if the mortgage ends up worth more than the property? The lender has no recourse if the value of the property drops below the total accrued principal and interest on the mortgage.

Where's the catch?

None of this is as attractive to a lender as a regular mortgage, so don't expect to get the interest rate or the loan amount you would receive if you were a new purchaser — at least, not right after retirement. The older you are, the sooner the mortgage company can expect to see its money back; hence, the better the deal they can offer you. Before you sign up for a reverse mortgage, take the time to get some legal advice and consider it carefully.

Summary

The different ways in which retirees finance their non-working years are as different as the retirees themselves. Most retirees draw their income from four main sources: RRSPs and RRIFs, non-registered investments, company pensions, and government support. If you are a homeowner and looking for extra retirement income, it may be right under your nose. If it makes financial sense for you, consider selling your empty nest and moving into a smaller home, or taking out a reverse mortgage. You have worked long and hard to get to your retirement. You are entitled to get as much out of it as you can!

QUICK RECAP

1. Know your sources of retirement income and how to draw on them in the most tax-effective way.

2. A careful mix of investments can help protect you against inflation.

3. If you don't have enough resources to fund your retirement, you may want to consider a reverse mortgage.

CHAPTER 4

Making the Best Choice at 69

Meeting the RRSP Conversion Deadline

It's crucial to plan ahead for the RRSP conversion deadline: the date by which an owner of an RRSP must convert it into a RRIF or annuity to provide a retirement income. Under the Income Tax Act, you must decide what to do with your RRSP by December 31 of the year you turn 69.

Above all, don't miss the deadline; if you do, you'll get the tax shock of your life. In the eyes of Revenue Canada, all assets of your plan are deregistered and are regarded as income earned that year — and are taxed accordingly. Neglecting to fill out one simple form could cost you half of your nest egg. Though financial institutions are trying their best to alert their clients who will be affected by the deadline, many people still haven't gotten the message. Don't let the worst happen to you.

Keep in mind that it takes time to plan for wise decisions on how best to convert your RRSPs. Seek professional advice a few months earlier to allow ample time.

RRSP Rollover

There are several options for what to do with your RRSP as you reach 69 — RRIFs, life annuities, and term-certain annuities.

If you are recently retired and planning ahead for your RRSP conversion, you may still have a few years to go. You should meet with a financial advisor to talk over RRIFs and annuities. Among other issues, you should explore how best to keep your money tax sheltered in the future. Don't wait until 69 candles are flickering on your birthday cake to look into which options are best for you.

THE CONVERSION DEADLINE

The most important information in this book: if you miss the deadline for converting your RRSP into a RRIF or other retirement income options, the money in your RRSP will probably be fully taxable. MISSING THE DEADLINE COULD COST YOU UP TO HALF OF YOUR NEST-EGG with no avenue for appeal.

The RRIF Route

It's easy to see why most people choose a RRIF for their retirement income. A RRIF is an investment vehicle and a tax shelter, just as your RRSP is. RRIFs allow you to invest in all the same securities RRSPs do: mutual funds, guaranteed investment certificates (GICs), bonds, etc. You get to keep 20 percent invested in foreign content for maximum diversification, just as you do with an RRSP. The big difference between an RRSP and a RRIF is that you must withdraw a certain minimum amount annually from a RRIF as retirement income.

Money left in a RRIF when you die becomes part of your estate and is subject to tax on your final tax return, unless it is transferred to your spouse's RRIF or RRSP.

Locked-in RRSPs

Locked-in RRSPs contain money that was transferred from pension plans, and are subject to pension legislation restrictions. They have a prescribed payout formula that must be followed. (The only exception is if you suffer from a severe disability that is likely to shorten your life expectancy.) Locked-in RRSPs can be converted to annuities, Life Income Funds (LIFs), or in some provinces Locked-in Retirement Income Funds (LRIFs).

Investments within the RRIF, LIF, or LRIF

Consider the following savings and investment vehicles. A savings account pays the lowest interest rates — not a good place to park your money. A GIC pays a fixed interest rate; however, your flexibility is limited. A mutual fund offers more flexibility and greater opportunity for investment performance, but more risk. A self-directed plan allows you to include your own choices from a range of options. You can select bonds and bond funds, money market funds, stocks, mutual funds, GICs, etc. For more information on investment strategies and vehicles, see Chapters 7 and 8.

Becoming Your Own RRIF Manager

You probably know that RRIFs are administered through financial institutions, but did you know that you can manage your own RRIF portfolio? A self-directed RRIF involves more work than having a manager look out for your money, and you are entirely responsible for doing your own research and monitoring investments outside of any mutual fund investments. But for some people, they offer a great feeling of accomplishment.

Moreover, some types of investments are open only to self-directed RRIF holders. Be warned though: you have to know what you are doing and what types of investments are available to you, as well as keep abreast of changes that the government makes to RRIF rules. There is no investment advisor or money manager to hold your hand with these plans, so your risk is greater.

Self-directed plans generally have fees attached, often $100 to $150 per plan every year.

Handling Withdrawals

Planning the withdrawal schedule for your RRIF? This is a good time to seek professional advice, since needs and formulas vary widely. Some people choose to take out more than the minimum in the earlier years of their retirement, when they're traveling or want to enjoy time at a second home. Other people would rather leave as much money as possible in the fund for later, in case high medical or personal expenses crop up. Contrary to popular belief, there's a minimum but no set rate you have to use. And, if you find your planned withdrawal schedule isn't the best one for you, you can always change it later. The law only specifies the minimum annual required withdrawals. You can take out as much as you like, subject to a minimum requirement (as long as it's not a LIF or LRIF).

However, the beauty of the RRIF is that it allows your money to keep growing in those tax-deferred conditions.

Withdrawing it early only works against this goal, as with-drawals are taxable in the year they are made. RRIF regula-tions allow couples to base withdrawals on the younger spouse's age. If you are married, make sure you always do this, since it keeps the tax advantage in place as long as pos-sible. Make it clear when you set up the RRIF that you intend to go by the younger person's age. The taxable annual mini-mum withdrawals are based on your age (or your spouse's) on January 1 of that year.

RRIF withdrawal rules changed in 1993, when the federal government decided to let plans continue after people reached age 90. Plans that predate this change and operate under the old rules will do so until the holder (or younger spouse) reach-es 78, at which time the amended RRIF minimums take effect. These plans' minimum withdrawals are, to age 78, somewhat lower than those of newer plans. Contact your financial advi-sor for the specific minimum RRIF withdrawal rules that apply to you.

Note this important administrative detail: while most self-directed RRIF fees can be paid either from outside the plan or from within it, charges related to management of securities (investment counseling, for example, or commissions) must be paid with money from the plan.

Summary

So of the two types of tax-sheltered plans available to retirees, — RRIFs or annuities — which should you choose? Planning your retirement income and investments is not a simple task. Speak with a financial planning professional who can help you set up the plan that is best for you. Do it earlier rather than waiting until the last minute.

QUICK RECAP

1. Plan ahead for the RRSP conversion deadline.

2. Choose the right conversion vehicle for you: RRIFs or annuities or a combination of both.

CHAPTER 5

Home Is Where the Heart Is

Lloyd, the retired widower, wants to enjoy every minute of his retirement and he doesn't want to have to live on the cheap. But before he knows how much he can afford to spend enjoying life in the upcoming years, Lloyd needs to assess how much he is currently worth. Lloyd has decided to seriously look into buying that beachfront condo, with plenty of room for visiting family, and he sees owning a bit of tropical paradise as his incentive for sticking to the budget he prepared for himself and getting his credit rating under control.

Your Principal Residence — One of Your Biggest Assets

Many people think about selling their principal residence upon retirement. You may decide that you don't need all that space, and you could spend the money you make on a trip, on a winter home in Florida, or on other assets to make your retirement comfortable. But selling is not always the best option. Sure, you may walk away with $200,000 in your pocket, but what you're giving up can be worth more, both as cash and as a safety net to protect you as you get on in years. You have to live someplace, and why shouldn't that place be the home you're comfortable in?

Will a Condo Give You the High Life?

Some house owners consider selling their houses and buying condos when they reach retirement. For many people, condos provide the lifestyle and the freedom they want. Many condo developments are geared specifically toward retired people, which can mean a whole new social life. Also, condo corporations usually take care of maintenance, letting you travel without worrying about your home. If you own a condo, you will have fewer security worries: the probability of break-ins is greatly reduced. Also, you may have indoor parking, no driveway to shovel, and no grass to cut.

Think over the benefits and drawbacks before you make your decision. Condo living is not for everyone, and getting older doesn't mean giving up what is important to you. Are you ready to give up your garden if your condo is in a highrise, or your neighbours, if they have become your friends over the years? Condo life can seem simple, since upkeep is taken care of, but the maintenance fees can be steep when you think about how little it costs to hire a student or to have your kids come over and help paint the house or mow the lawn. One final financial consideration: whereas your house usually increases in value each year, some condos can decrease in value.

Home Equity Borrowing

If you have ever bought a house, you'll already be familiar with mortgages. But if you're thinking of purchasing a vacation home, you may find a mortgage more difficult to obtain and the down payment and loan rates likely higher. An alternative is to mortgage the equity on your house to finance buying a cottage or recreational property.

You can take this loan as a fixed or variable personal loan or as a variable line of credit. The lender sets a limit on how much you can borrow (usually not more than 75 percent of the appraised value) and sets the repayment terms. If you are making a large purchase, such as a cottage or ski chalet, you may wish to take the entire loan all at once through a personal loan. But if you are using your home equity to finance smaller purchases, such as home renovations or vehicles, you might want to take a personal line of credit so that you can access funds only as you need them, rather than having to pay interest on a large loan that you are not using all at once.

Remaining a Home Owner

Inflation protection

If you don't own a home, you're likely renting, which means that your rent will go up every year to meet the costs of inflation. That rent will only build your landlord's net worth, not your own.

Owning your home, however, gives you shelter from the constant buffetting of inflation. Your mortgage payments remain constant over the term of your mortgage, and only interest rates change. If your home is paid off, it may be tempting to take the money and run, but staying in your home may, in fact, give you more freedom. Once the mortgage is paid off, your only expenses will be household bills and taxes. Although you may be reluctant to ever call yourself a senior, there are certain breaks on property taxes available to seniors. Some tax breaks are also available to renters, but they tend to be fewer and smaller.

Shelter for your old age

Retirement homes are becoming increasingly expensive. Your home — more specifically the equity you have in it — could be a potentially tax-free pool of capital if you should ever need to move to a retirement home. Unless the real estate market takes a dive, your home should continue to appreciate in value until you need to move.

Shelter for your taxes

If you bought a house years ago, you've probably seen a great increase in its value. So if you do finally decide to sell, you'll be able to profit from the capital gains tax exemption on your principal residence. If your house was your principal residence for as long as you owned it, any gain you make from the sale goes into your pocket, tax free. Your principal residence can be whatever you call home, whether that's a suburban bungalow, a vacation property, a century-old schoolhouse that you fixed up, a houseboat, or a trailer. Or, if you rent an apartment in the city but own a vacation property where you live for part of the year, your vacation property can be considered your principal residence.

If you purchased your vacation property after January 1, 1982, you can't claim the tax exemption on both your house and your vacation property. A family unit can claim only one

KEEP YOUR VALUES IN MIND

Studies show that most people want the same things in retirement that they did when they were working. Maybe your day-to-day life changes, but your values and your chosen lifestyle probably won't. Think about your lifelong values before deciding to sell your home and move to a rental property. Will it mean moving away from family and friends? Will you have to sell some of those treasured antiques you inherited from your mother? Can you picture yourself as a condo dweller? Take a look at all your options before deciding what is best for you. Maybe moving to a smaller bungalow that needs fixing up will give you the lifestyle you want, as well as a new project to work on.

owner-occupied property. If you owned two properties before 1982, you may be entitled to some additional capital gains exemptions. Get professional advice on your taxes if this applies to you.

Buying a Retirement Property

Canadians are well-known for being water fanatics, so it's not surprising that many people choose a vacation property as their retirement home. If you are considering buying a retirement home or making retirement a permanent holiday at the cottage you've had for years, you'll have a lot to think over. Access to both health care and cultural facilities is one thing. Resale value is another. (If you haven't tried country living before, you may wish to rent a country home for a few months, just to make sure that living close to nature is really for you.)

Retiring to the Vacation Property

You've already done your net worth assessment, so now see if running a second household fits into your financial plan.

If you keep your city home, can you afford to pay insurance and taxes on two properties? You might think that school tax, for example, doesn't apply in remote areas that don't even have schools, but surprise! School taxes apply to many vacation properties. Can you afford the cost of upkeep? Think about how much you spend on average each year maintaining your house, then add 50 percent to that number. Vacation properties tend to be more exposed to the elements, so they'll require painting and roof repairs every few years. Also, they are often less structurally sound. A home that hasn't been lived in for much of the year is probably not as well maintained as a home in urban areas. If you're buying an existing vacation property, is it winterized? Many retirees make their vacation homes their primary residences, which can involve having a vacation property insulated and heated. Does it offer the comforts that you are used to, and will increasingly depend upon as you age: hydro, dependable and drinkable water, a septic system that can withstand year-round use, a road that's cleared in the win-

DO YOUR HOMEWORK

Whatever type of retirement residence you're thinking about buying, be sure to do your homework. Ask your real estate agent a lot of questions and talk to neighbours. Find out what the community has to offer you, whether it is in the country or the city. Consider some of the doubling-up costs of buying a second home as a retirement residence:

1. Can you afford the insurance and the taxes?
2. Can you afford double the cost of upkeep?
3. If you couldn't drive, is there any other way to get there?

ter, telephone lines, and perhaps cable or satellite TV? If not, what will it cost to bring the vacation property up to your standard of living?

The list goes on and on and on, but these are just a few of the issues that can have a major impact on your finances.

Joining the Snowbirds

As you grow older, the Canadian winter seems to grow longer, and winter sports such as mogul skiing and ice skating start to lose their appeal. That's why many people's retirement plans include living outside of Canada, in a warmer climate, for at least part of the year. During these extended stays in another country, most people choose to rent a furnished condominium or time-share, rather than stay in a hotel. Renting offers the same freedom and convenience of living in your own home and is usually more affordable than staying in a hotel.

Although some retire to the warm climates of the Mediterranean, Costa Rica, or Mexico, most migrating retirees wish to move to a country fairly similar to their own, where people speak the same language as they do and the social customs are familiar. Many opt for the comfort of the southern United States. Canadians have made retirement homes for themselves from California to Florida and everywhere in between.

Cost-of-Living Benefits

Living in a warmer country for part of your retirement can sometimes lower your cost of living. It is expensive to live in Canada, for many reasons, some of which stem from our tax system, our social benefits, and many of which stem from our climate, over which we have no control. If you live in Florida or Arizona, it may be warm all year-round and you won't have to buy snow tires, but you have to contend with the often-terrible exchange rate. It can be very expensive living in the United States if every dollar you spend is worth only 70 cents.

Keeping Your Canadian Residency

If you live in another country part of the year, you may choose to retain your Canadian residency status, which would allow you to keep all of the rights and privileges of being a Canadian. This is important to some retirees because it means that they can still use the Canadian health care system, to which their taxes contributed during their working years. Qualifications for Canadian residency are not hard and fast, but essentially, to remain a Canadian resident for tax purposes, you must keep a home here and live in Canada for more than half of every year. If you plan to live elsewhere for more than six months a year and retain your Canadian residency, you must maintain strong ties to Canada through real estate, bank accounts, investments, and club memberships. In this case, your residency status for tax purposes is determined by how much you continue to be involved in your Canadian affairs. U.S. immigration rules will prohibit you from spending more than six months in the U.S.

Under certain circumstances, the U.S. will also require you to complete forms each year to prove that you are a resident of Canada for tax purposes. The U.S. government uses a complex formula, so contact a professional advisor.

Giving Up Canadian Residency

Many Canadian retirees choose to become non-residents of Canada and take up full-time residency in the United States. The North American Free Trade Agreement has made moving to the U.S. somewhat easier.

MAKE YOUR DECISION WITH CONFIDENCE

Deciding where to live in your retirement means being as informed as possible about the financial and personal implications of your choices. For more information on the financial consequences, read Revenue Canada's publication *Living Outside Canada* and speak to your financial advisor.

If you are considering moving somewhere new, find out what the community is really like and think about renting there for a few months before you decide. Subscribe to local newspapers, ask the tourism office for brochures, and talk with residents. Wading through this information may seem time consuming, but the more information you have, the more confident you will be in making your decision.

Although becoming a U.S. resident restricts the amount of time each year that you may spend in Canada, visiting family and friends or vacationing, there may be some good reasons for choosing this option.

Receiving Canadian Benefits in the United States

Canada has certain agreements with the United States that enable Canadians to receive most of their Canadian social security benefits, with the notable exception of health care, when they become residents of the United States. If you do become a U.S. resident, make sure you purchase health care coverage, as the United States doesn't have universal medical care.

Two social security benefits that Canadian seniors receive are OAS and CPP/QPP payments. Luckily, you are entitled to both of these benefits if you become a resident of the United

States in your retirement. Quite simply, if you were entitled to OAS before moving to the United States, it will be mailed to you at your new address. CPP/QPP benefits, which are paid to people no matter where they move or how long they lived in Canada, are also sent directly to your home in the United States.

Buying a Home Outside of Canada

No retirement book would be complete without comments on buying property in the sunbelt. Florida is practically becoming another province, with all of the Canadians who are choosing to live there during the winter. We've discussed the effect that living in the United States has on your taxes and health care. For now, think about whether buying or renting is your best choice.

Unless you plan on spending most of the year there, it may be a better idea to rent rather than buy your sunbelt home. You may not want to tie up a lot of money in a home that you won't be using for much of the year. Trying to sell a property in one country from another country also can be a hassle. The sunbelt tends to be overdeveloped, so although you can buy a home for a song, you also might end up selling it for a pittance.

Renting out property you've purchased in the United States is one way to get around the expense of running a home that is empty for much of the year. But renting can be complicated in terms of taxes. Your tenants will have to direct 30 percent of their rent to the IRS as withholding tax on your behalf unless you file a United States tax return. Each year you must file a tax return to report your rental income minus net expenses, such as maintenance fees.

If you decide to sell your property in the United States, the IRS may withhold 10 percent of the selling price, regardless of whether you sell at a profit or a loss. You'll have to file a United States tax return to report the sale of your property, and United States capital gains tax is applicable if you sell at a profit. If the tax withheld is greater than the ultimate tax liability, the difference is refunded upon filing the return. There are steps you can take to reduce the withholding tax if the ultimate tax liability will be less.

The U.S. could levy estate tax on any property you own at the time of your death.

It's a good idea to get professional advice from an accountant who deals with United States–Canada tax laws. An accountant may even be able to assist you in having the 10 percent withholding tax reduced or eliminated.

Helping to Lower Your Income Taxes

Giving up Canadian residency can have an impact on your taxes. If you become a resident of another country, you will be taxed at that country's rate, which can sometimes work to your advantage, since Canadians are heavily taxed in general, and taxes are usually lower in sunbelt areas.

Keep in mind that as a resident of another country you will be subject to the tax laws of that country and maybe even to state, provincial, and city tax. If you move to a new country, you should consult a specialist in that country's taxes.

Canada still has the right to withhold tax on Canadian-source income. The tax rate may be reduced if there is a tax treaty with the country in which you take up residence, and you may get credit for that withholding tax in your new location. It is possible that the combination of the withholding tax on that Canadian source income, and the taxes imposed by your new country of residence, will be less than if you had remained a Canadian resident. Some common examples are:

- If you are a resident of a country other than Canada, periodic payments from a RRIF are subject to withholding tax at rates up to 25 percent and little or no tax in the country to which you move. In Canada, you could be taxed on up to 53 percent of the same amount.
- Canada may withhold tax on OAS and CPP/QPP depending on where you've moved to. However, the Canada–United States tax treaty provides that only the United States can tax OAS and CPP/QPP payments to residents of the United States. This may result in lower tax on those items and may be a way to avoid the OAS clawback.

Summary

How and where you live during your retirement is a personal decision: some people are more attached to their homes (and friends and family!) than others, while the first priority for some people is to move far away from Canada's long winters. While your decision of where to live should be based on your goals and values, don't forget about the practical side of things. Look into the costs of living in various locations before you decide — taxes and cost of living vary widely from Canada to the United States, and living at your cottage may be cheaper than living in a city. This is a big decision, look at it from all angles.

QUICK RECAP

1. Decide how important it is to you to keep your current home in your retirement.

2. Be aware of the ups and downs to living in a warmer climate.

3. Look for ways to lower your taxes no matter where you live.

CHAPTER **6**

Good Debt, Bad Debt

Seeing as Laszlo and Sally are going to be spending a lot more time at home together, they want to do some renovations and buy a few items to make their home more comfortable. They met with a financial advisor because they were unsure which of their investments they should use to pay for the new furniture and building materials. It seemed no matter which investment they chose, they would be looking at much higher taxes this year. Their advisor suggested that they use their line of credit to finance the renovations until they can use their investments in a tax-effective way.

Financing Your Household Assets

Now that you've figured out what's important to your retirement lifestyle, you'll need to think about how you can make those dreams a reality by financing them. Perhaps you've decided to buy an RV and tour the continent, or maybe you'd like to buy a boat and just drift for a while. Whatever choice you make, you'll want it to be a financially sound one that won't eat away at the income that has to last you through retirement. Take a look at the following kinds of financing, and then decide which one is right for you.

Pay Cash

If you've got extra cash lying around, or a liquid investment (a GIC, for example) that's unspoken for, this is the option for you. Immediately paying for part or all of a big-ticket item reduces your expenses in the long run because you won't be paying off interest on borrowed money.

What Kind of Loan Do You Need?

Lines of credit

A line of credit is a type of demand loan that is approved for your unspecified use. Once approved, you can access the line of credit at any time, up to the predetermined limit, with special cheques or a credit card. A normal starting limit for a line of credit is $5,000. Many people find it convenient to pay for high-ticket items, such as home improvements, vacations, recreational equipment, or even investments, with a line of credit. The terms of repayment are set in advance, and interest rates are better than the rates on an unpaid credit card balance. You are charged interest only on the portion you have used. So you can let it sit until you really need it. Once you use it, though, the lender will calculate the interest daily and charge you monthly.

Good Debt, Bad Debt

Good debt is debt that you undertake to make money — to invest in stocks, for example. When you borrow to make an investment, the interest is usually tax deductible as long as the loan proceeds are invested in an income-producing asset. Credit card debt is only good for you if you manage to pay off the full balance each month. That's the kind of debt that boosts your credit rating.

Bad debt is the kind that you incur without getting anything valuable in return. Not paying off your credit cards at the due date is bad debt — double trouble because it also means you haven't budgeted properly and are living beyond your means. Carrying a lot of high-cost long-term debt means paying a lot of interest charges. Sometimes the interest can add up to many times the amount of the original loan. So look into ways to pay down your debt before it becomes a mountain.

Paying Off Bad Debt

Okay, so you're not perfect and you have managed to acquire bad debt. There are sensible ways to manage that undesirable debt.

- Prioritize your debts by paying off non-tax-deductible high-interest debt, such as credit card balances, before low-interest debt.
- See if you are eligible for a credit card with a lower rate of interest and transfer your high-interest balance to the new card.
- Get rid of extra credit cards. After all, how many do you really need?
- Beware of retailer credit cards. Retailers charge huge amounts of interest, usually about 28 percent, and they accept most major credit cards, anyway.

- Consider dipping into your savings account or Canada Savings Bonds to pay off high-interest debt. The after-tax interest you lose on the cash or the bonds can be much less than the money you gain by retiring your unpaid credit card balance.
- Pull out your budget again, and see if you can reduce your spending.
- Start paying with cash or by debit card. This way, you will know exactly how much you can spend and you will get into the habit of living within your means.

Credit Cards

Four reasons why you, as a retiree, should carry credit cards:

1. prepaid travel or rental insurance
2. a line of credit for emergencies
3. bonus points or discounts
4. identification when writing cheques

YOUR CREDIT RATING NEVER RETIRES

Your credit rating sums up your reputation as a borrower. It evaluates your debt in the past six years and in the present.

Keep these numbers on file so that you can check your credit rating if you need to:

Equifax Canada Inc.: Call 1-800-465-7166 or (in Toronto) 416-590-8700.
Trans-Union of Canada Inc.: Call 905-525-4420.

Summary: Make Debt Work for You

For many people, retirement means not slowing down but actually doing more. Now that you have the time, you may decide to take up sailing, golf, or vacationing in Arizona at a retirement community. However you decide to spend your time, it's possible you may occasionally need to use debts to fund your retirement goals. There are right ways and wrong ways to use debt. If you play your cards right and manage your debts, your retirement can be active and worry free.

QUICK RECAP

1. **Don't deprive yourself in retirement — but buy assets wisely.**

2. **Manage your debt: out with the bad debt and in with the good.**

CHAPTER 7

Smart Investing

Lloyd has always loved the thrill of investing his money and playing with penny stocks. But often it was just a game — he'd win big and lose big and usually ended up right where he began. His wife suggested that he get mutual funds a long time ago and he has a company pension, but other than that his investments are very high-risk and speculative. When his wife died, he didn't get any more conservative in his investing style. Now that he is retired and has some concrete plans for spending his money, Lloyd can't afford to lose anything to an uncertain stock market. In order to figure out how to redistribute his portfolio and to learn about some new investment options, Lloyd decided to talk to a financial advisor.

Everyone Needs a Strategy

Even a loonie in a piggybank loses value to inflation. But smart investing allows you to beat inflation by making that loonie worth more rather than less. Investing your money in the right place can give you financial security, increase your net worth, and take you many steps toward financial independence. You can set a sound investment strategy by understanding the characteristics of different types of investments and creating the right balanced mix of investments that helps your money grow and lets you sleep at night. Your best way of developing that strategy is doing it with the help of a professional financial advisor.

Selecting a Financial Advisor

Financial advisors take the time to know the lifestyle and financial needs of their clients. They have invested their time and energy into becoming knowledgeable in investments, taxation, estate planning, insurance, and retirement planning. In addition, they may work with a network of specialists who can provide the in-depth knowledge needed to deal with situations as they arise. Search for a financial advisor who combines an understanding of people with knowledge of technical planning matters. Most will provide you an opportunity to learn about the processes they use and will give detailed information on the services they offer and the company they work for before expecting you to begin the financial planning process. Things to look for in choosing an advisor:

- You feel compatible with the advisor and feel you can work well together.
- The advisor has an appropriate educational background.
- The advisor belongs to a professional association that has a code of ethics and standards.
- The advisor works for an established, solid financial institution.
- The advisor is willing to explain how he or she comes to a complete understanding of your current and desired personal and family financial situation.

- The same advisor who meets with you initially will continue to work on all of your subsequent needs.
- The advisor will review your situation at least annually.
- The advisor fully reveals how he or she is compensated for working on your account.

Know Yourself

When you review your investment portfolio, you'll have to do some soul searching to match your investment mix to your goals and time frame. Ask yourself first about your time horizon and risk tolerance. What is the worst-case scenario? Remember, it is always a good idea to have a professional advisor help you through this process. Take stock of who and where you are, where you want to go, and how long you have to get there. Find out what sort of risk you are comfortable with.

- *Attitude:* Are you the kind of person who lies awake worrying about whether your financial institution will be struck by lightning? If so, you probably won't tolerate a lot of risk in your investment portfolio, and you'd be better off investing your money conservatively.
- *Age:* How old are you? The further into your retirement you are, the more conservative your portfolio should be.
- *Responsibilities:* Who or what depends on your retirement income? If you still have dependants, a mortgage, or a loan to support, you probably can't afford to take great risk, so you'll want to invest your money conservatively.
- *Cash flow:* What's your retirement income stream like? What kind of investments do you have? Are you receiving a company pension plan? How much government support are you getting? If your cash flow is erratic or likely to decrease, you don't want to invest in anything volatile.

- *Desired rate of return:* Different assets have different risk levels and therefore different potential rates of return.

Assessing Your Risk Tolerance

Only you know your attitude toward risk, so you must assess your own comfort zone. Ask yourself "What's the worst that can happen if this doesn't work?" If "the worst" is something you can live with, then the risk is acceptable. Keep in mind that there is risk in not investing at all, or in investing where after-tax returns are less than inflation. The risk is that your purchasing power will decrease.

Smart investing means having the appropriate balance of different investments to provide long-term growth with a risk level that is acceptable to you. The longer you have until you need the money, the more you can use investments with higher variability. This is because historically markets have tended to climb over time, while experiencing peaks and valleys. The mix and balance of your investment portfolio will evolve as you get closer to the time you need the money.

In determining what risk is acceptable to you, keep in mind your short- and long-term goals. If you are planning to buy a second home next year, you don't want to put your down payment money into the stock market now, no matter how high it's soaring. A market downturn that coincides with your purchase date would have a serious impact on your short-term goal.

Although assessing your risk tolerance is largely a personal matter, some principles apply to just about everyone. For example, a 60-year-old can tolerate more investment fluctuation than a 75-year-old. The closer you are to needing your nest egg, the less you're going to want to have in more volatile investments. One very rough way of calculating this "age/risk ratio" is to subtract your age from 100. The number left over will be the percentage that you can afford to put in higher-return, higher-risk investments, such as equities. So if you're 65, 35 percent of your investment portfolio might be in equities. As you get older, this percentage will shrink. An advisor can help you make a more calculated decision on your investment portfolio mix.

How Your Portfolio Should Change in Retirement

Just because you've retired doesn't mean your portfolio should. But your investment needs will evolve. You may have been able to afford an aggressive investment strategy in the past, but you need to consider changing the balance of your portfolio to suit your changing risk tolerance.

If you're 65-years-old and retired, you may need to finance another 20 to 25 years of your life. At this stage of the game, inflation's your greatest enemy. Managing your portfolio is the best way to stave off the effects of inflation once you've retired. As a general rule, the older you are, the lower the equity component of your investment portfolio should be. However, in retirement, you should invest a certain percentage of your assets in equity investments to offset inflation. By putting too much of your retirement funds into fixed income investments and certificates of deposit you could miss out on market surges that would swell your savings. You also need to be sure that your fixed investments are working for you. Be sure the yield is positive after your taxes and inflation have been deducted. Keep in mind that it's important to find a good balance that's right for your situation.

Risk Tolerance and Retirement

Risk means different things to different people. Here is a relative yardstick for investment risk that can help you decide where your emotional comfort level is.

Very low: Your only concern is for the security of your investment.

Low: You could tolerate a fluctuation of no more than 10 percent in the value of your investment, occurring rarely, and even this would make you uncomfortable.

Moderate: You would not be upset about a fluctuation of 10 to 20 percent in the value of your investment, as long as you would eventually benefit from a positive return.

High: You could handle a fluctuation of 20 to 50 percent in the value of your investment provided there's still hope for a positive return sometime in the future.

Very High: You could tolerate a fluctuation of 50 percent or more in the value of your investment as long as you'd see a healthy return in the future.

Most people in the over-60 age group often have either low or very low risk tolerance because they have less time to make up for a decrease in the value of their portfolio due to a market down cycle. For that reason, investments like GICs, bonds, and mortgage funds, which are both income earning and low risk, are popular. But the younger and healthier you are, the further your money has to stretch. For that reason, too high a proportion of income investments could lead to erosion of your portfolio by inflation.

Managing Risk

You can't and shouldn't avoid risk altogether, but you can manage it. It is rather like driving a car on a highway. There's always some risk of accident or injury, but you can "manage" the risk by wearing a seatbelt, driving at a sensible speed, ensuring that the car is well maintained, and so on. You can reduce the risk even further by not making the trip or by never leaving your home.

Similarly, you can reduce the risk of investment losses to near zero by keeping your money under your mattress, but that increases the risk of losing purchasing power to inflation. You shouldn't fret about investment risk. The key is to understand the risks and, with the help of a professional advisor, build a portfolio that has the right level and mix of investments appropriate for you. You should, however, be aware of the different kinds of risk and how they affect different investments in different ways.

Inflation risk. This is a special concern for GICs and other "risk-free" investments. If, for example, inflation is 3 percent, a GIC at 5 percent will give a real return of only 2 percent and you likely will have lost purchasing power after tax. Unless they are held in an RRSP or RRIF, you must also pay tax on GIC interest annually.

Interest rate risk. As interest rates rise, the market value of bonds falls. This is a concern if you have to sell a bond before it matures.

Currency risk. Fluctuating exchange rates can cut into (or increase) your return on investments made in foreign markets.

Economic risk. Certain industries are very sensitive to fluctuations in the economy. The auto industry tends to do well in good times. Others, including utilities such as electrical power and telecommunications, are less sensitive to economic cycles.

Industry risk. With the rapid pace of technological change, some industries, such as the computer industry, are inherently volatile.

Company risk. When you own a stock, you own part of a business, and even businesses in booming industries can be poorly managed.

Credit risk. If you're buying bonds, you're lending money to a company or government. Interest payments could be suspended or you may not be repaid your principal if the borrower runs into financial difficulty.

Liquidity risk. How easy is it to get your money with minimal capital loss? A bank account is liquid. Real estate is less liquid because you can't sell it until you find a buyer.

Political risk. Governments change the rules.

Evaluating the Performance of Your Investments

The press have a lot to say about the performance of investments, particularly mutual funds. Sensational headlines with this week's tragedies and tomorrow's predictions abound. When evaluating your investments — either over your morning newspaper and coffee, or formally with your financial advisor — be sure to follow these three simple rules:

Compare apples to apples. A mutual fund containing Pacific Rim stocks is much more volatile than one containing mortgages. They are different asset classes, with different risks and serving different purposes in your investment plan. As you can see from the table on the next page, the best and worst one-year periods for these investments vary widely.

There are no crystal balls. No one could have predicted what day you should have invested in order to have "ridden the wave" to the one-year 129.5% return on Japenese stocks. If that sort of prediction were possible, everyone would also have avoided the single-year losses of −42.1% in the same market! Your best bet is to be in a mix of asset classes, all of the time. That's why mutual funds make such excellent sense for most investors and why it's so important to include foreign content in your long-term RRSP.

Time reduces risk. The one-year highs and lows in the table demonstrate the relative volatility of each asset class. The average five-year returns demonstrate how time invested in a particular market or asset class reduced that level of volatility. Be patient if you can.

CASH & CASH EQUIVALENTS

	HIGHEST 1-YEAR RETURN	LOWEST 1-YEAR RETURN	AVERAGE 5-YEAR ANNUAL RETURN
Savings accounts	11.6%	0.5%	5.3%
90-day deposits	14.0%	4.5%	9.1%
Canada Savings Bonds	19.1%	5.1%	9.4%
5-year GICs	14.8%	5.8%	10.0%

FIXED INCOME INVESTMENTS

	HIGHEST 1-YEAR RETURN	LOWEST 1-YEAR RETURN	AVERAGE 5-YEAR ANNUAL RETURN
Mortgages	34.8%	–2.0%	11.7%
Bonds	55.6%	–10.4%	13.7%
Dividend Stocks	79.5%	–14.5%	12.5%
Real Estate	19.3%	–7.1%	7.5%

EQUITY INVESTMENTS

	HIGHEST 1-YEAR RETURN	LOWEST 1-YEAR RETURN	AVERAGE 5-YEAR ANNUAL RETURN
Canadian Index	86.9%	–18.5%	9.7%
U.S. Index	56.9%	–22.8%	15.7%
Japanese Index	129.5%	–42.1%	15.6%
World Index	63.5%	–23.2%	13.0%
European Index	111.5%	–23.2%	17.1%

INFLATION

	HIGHEST 1-YEAR RATE	LOWEST 1-YEAR RATE	AVERAGE 5-YEAR RATE
Consumer Price Index	8.3%	–0.2%	3.7%

Notes. This table contains historical data and there is no assurance that future results will be consistent with this table. All rates of return occurred during the period January 1, 1982 to December 31, 1996.

Developing an Investment Strategy

A sound investment strategy starts with a good understanding of your financial goals. One approach is to divide your assets into three "pots" — to meet short-, mid-, and long-term goals. An example of a long-term goal is to create an investment portfolio that will keep your retirement income steady for the next 20 years or longer. A mid-term goal is to replace your car in five years. A short-term goal is to fund the down payment on a vacation property next summer. Assume only as much risk as you need to meet each goal.

Money from each "pot" can be distributed among three classes of investments:

- cash or cash equivalents, meaning liquid investments, such as government savings bonds, T-bills, and money market funds;
- fixed-income securities, which pay a fixed income and are held for a term of over a year, such as GICs, and fixed-income mutual funds; and
- equity investments, which can potentially provide the highest gains, but which also come with the greatest volatility, including Canadian and international stocks, and equity mutual funds.

Think of your portfolio as being made up of both your RRSPs/RRIFs and your other investments, which are probably not tax-sheltered. In your short-term pot, you will want to have most of your investments in fixed income and cash equivalents. In your long-term pot, you should include more variable investments, such as Canadian and foreign equities, to achieve bigger rewards. The medium-term pot will contain a balance of the two.

Building a Portfolio

To tailor your portfolio to your own investment needs, ask yourself the following questions:

- How much do I need to keep available for emergencies and short-term goals?
- How much do I need to invest for the long term?
- Will I benefit more from a compounding rate of return or do I need income from my investments?

- What are the tax consequences of my investment?
- How much variability am I willing to accept?

Your investment strategy should consist of dividing your assets in such a way that your investments are diversified. This strategy is called asset allocation. The strategy involves building a portfolio that includes assets from each of the three asset categories (cash, fixed income, and equity), from the Canadian market as well as international markets. How much you invest

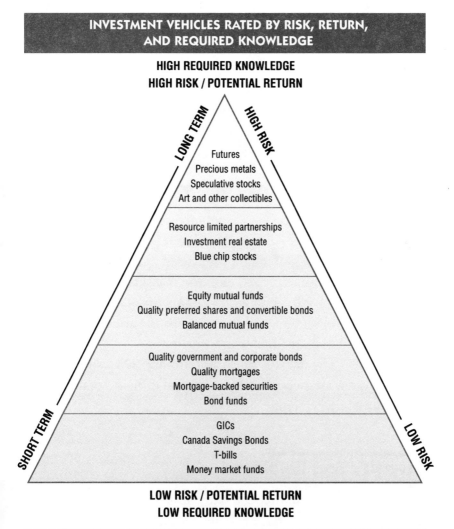

INVESTMENT VEHICLES RATED BY RISK, RETURN, AND REQUIRED KNOWLEDGE

HIGH REQUIRED KNOWLEDGE
HIGH RISK / POTENTIAL RETURN

LONG TERM / *HIGH RISK*

Futures
Precious metals
Speculative stocks
Art and other collectibles

Resource limited partnerships
Investment real estate
Blue chip stocks

Equity mutual funds
Quality preferred shares and convertible bonds
Balanced mutual funds

Quality government and corporate bonds
Quality mortgages
Mortgage-backed securities
Bond funds

GICs
Canada Savings Bonds
T-bills
Money market funds

SHORT TERM / *LOW RISK*

LOW RISK / POTENTIAL RETURN
LOW REQUIRED KNOWLEDGE

in each category is determined by your tolerance for risk and your time horizon. Peaks in the performance of one category will tend to balance out valleys in another, and the overall result should be closer to steady growth than you would achieve by putting all your eggs in one basket. Most financial professionals agree that asset allocation — the correct proportion of stocks, bonds, and cash — is more important to total portfolio performance than picking the top performers.

If you suddenly wake up in a cold sweat on your 65th birthday and you realize that you haven't saved enough to maintain your lifestyle in retirement, don't panic and throw all your money into high-return, high-risk investments in the hope of making up for lost time. Without setting out a good strategy, you could end up losing more than you make. Make achieving a balance between risk and reward your highest priority, and you'll make the most of what you have.

As Markets Move — Stay the Course

Once you've developed your asset mix, review it at least annually and rebalance to maintain your desired asset mix. Remember, you are looking for long-term growth, so don't vary your asset mix with every move in the markets. An asset mix is also relatively easy to align with your age/risk ratio. When you are retired, you should adjust your mix toward fixed-income securities and cash, maintaining a smaller percentage in growth investments. The key is time, not timing. Don't tinker too often, and use an investment professional to help you build the right mix of investments.

Diversify Your Holdings

A successful asset mix depends not on being in the right market at the right time, but on being in most markets all of the time, with varying exposures. If you've created an asset mix for your investments, you've already diversified your holdings to a degree. Diversification, however, doesn't just mean putting money into different investment vehicles. Look into investments that will move some of your assets out of your community, and even out of Canada — our economy can take a downturn while others are on the rise. International mutual funds now make these investments feasible, even if you're not among the jet set.

Summary

Your investment portfolio is a personal thing, and should reflect you and your needs. The mix of investments you should hold during your retirement depends on factors such as your attitude, responsibilities, and your retirement goals. Working with a financial advisor is one way to feel secure about your investments. An advisor will help you learn about yourself by assessing what kind of investments are right for you, and show you how to build a diversified investment portfolio that suits your needs.

QUICK RECAP

1. **Find a professional financial advisor with whom you feel comfortable.**

2. **Build your portfolio around your risk tolerance, but remember that you can't avoid risk altogether.**

3. **Make sure that your portfolio is diversified.**

CHAPTER 8

Investment Vehicles

Types of Investments

In order to be an informed investor, you should understand what you're buying, what the investment is intended to do, and what the risks and tax consequences of your investment are. Let's get started by looking at the two basic categories of investments: debt and equity.

Debt investments

Governments, corporations, individuals, and other entities borrow money for a variety of purposes. These loans are called bonds. If you invest in one of these, you are the lender. You want to know:

- your prospects for getting your money back,
- what income you can expect while you hold the investment, and
- when and how you will receive both.

Debt instruments pay you interest. Once a bond is issued, it gains in value if interest rates drop, and vice versa; therefore, it may also provide capital gains or losses, which receive different tax treatment than interest.

Equity investments

These are usually shares in a company. They represent part ownership in the venture, with the prospect of all its risks and rewards. You need to know something about the company, its prospects, its market, and its competitors before you buy its shares. Equities offer the potential for capital gains and may pay dividends.

Variations on the Basics

There is a wide variety of investment products. The best-known and easiest to understand are mutual funds. But whatever investment you choose, there is always more to know about it than first appears. It's essential to stay informed and up to date. Choose your advisors well.

Time and timing

You can invest your money for periods ranging from less than 30 days to more than 30 years. Long-term debt instruments imply a forecast of inflation and interest rates for decades ahead — obviously something of a risk. If you're right, the rewards can be high. Some people still hold double-digit government bonds they bought when inflation was high. With stocks, the tendencies are reversed. They can be flipped in minutes, but that requires close attention and sometimes approaches gambling. Longer-term equity holdings are most consistently profitable. In general, short-term investing involves short-term management, which takes up more of your time — but any investment must be watched. It all boils down to when you buy the investment, how long you hold it, and when you sell it.

Value

When you're buying, selling, or trading investments, remember that the "value" of something — especially share equity — is not necessarily what you think it should be. It's no more than a buyer is willing to pay for it.

Looking into the Alternatives

What follows is a quick guide to the most common types of investments out there. They include debt and equity investments, and they have varying degrees of risk and reward. Read through these options and then talk them over with your financial advisor to decide which investments are right for you.

Types of Debt Investments

Interest or fixed-income investments

When you buy a fixed-income investment, your income is defined at the outset. It could be fixed or have different rates for different periods. You may receive your income when the term is up, or periodically over time. The same applies to your principal (if you invest in an amortized mortgage, for instance, with each payment you get some of your money back). If your risk tolerance is low, you'll want the majority of your investments in these vehicles. But don't expect to make your fortune this way. To calculate your real earnings, subtract taxes, then the rate of inflation. For example, suppose:

- your rate of return is 8 percent,
- you're in a 50 percent tax bracket, and
- inflation is 3 percent.

Your real rate of return is only 1 percent (8 − 4 − 3 = 1). Your tax rate will be determined by your income bracket. Assuming your borrower is reliable, your two greatest risks in a fixed-income investment are that inflation will wipe out your earnings (suppose, in the example, that inflation hits 5 percent or 6 percent), or that you'll be locked into a fixed return when current interest rates rise.

Canada Savings Bonds (CSBs)

- specific government bonds that cannot be traded, only kept or cashed in
- pay interest (after the first three months) to the end of the previous month
- interest income is fully taxable each year when held outside of an RRSP
- a safe and easy investment
- available at most financial institutions
- set at a fixed interest rate (which may change over the course of the term)
- easy to cash (high liquidity)
- available for as little as $100

Treasury bills (T-bills)

- government-issued investments that pay a specified return for a specified (usually short) period
- interest income is fully taxable each year when held outside of an RRSP
- safe; considered equivalent to cash
- issued by the Government of Canada and provincial governments for terms of 91, 182, and 364 days
- can be bought and sold at any time from banks and brokers
- defined rate of return
- usually sold in amounts from $5,000 to $25,000 or higher
- bought at a discount and mature at face value

THE CASE FOR GLOBAL DIVERSIFICATION

Canada and all of its investment opportunities represent only 3 percent of what the world has to offer. That means that an additional 97 percent of all opportunities exist outside of Canadian borders in stock and bond markets in different currencies around the globe.

While it's natural to feel most comfortable investing in our own back-yards, a more broad diversification can be achieved by including a cross section of investments from around the world.

Take advantage of foreign investment opportunities within your RRSP and RRIF — the government allows up to 20 percent of the book value of your registered plans to contain foreign holdings. One caution: you must be very careful to monitor the level of foreign content in your plan. There are penalties for exceeding the 20 percent mark.

Term deposits

- vehicles for depositing a fixed sum of money for a fixed period of time at a fixed or variable interest rate
- offered by most financial institutions
- usually carry a guaranteed rate of interest for the length of the term
- interest income is fully taxable each year when held outside of an RRSP
- not meant to be redeemed, so if redeemed, may be subject to penalties
- $500 minimum, usually invested for periods ranging from 30 to 364 days
- may be covered by federal deposit insurance (CDIC)
- a term deposit; of less than one year is called a certificate of deposit; anything longer is a GIC

Guaranteed investment certificates (GICs)

- interest-bearing deposits where interest can be paid periodically or upon maturity
- safe; covered by CDIC for up to $60,000 if purchased from an institution belonging to CDIC and the term is five years or less (If you have more than $60,000 to invest, buy from more than one insured institution.)
- interest income is fully taxable each year when held outside of an RRSP
- available at most financial institutions
- similar in structure and buying strategies to a term deposit
- cannot be traded; early redemption may be impossible or may involve penalties
- low minimums and limits, which are set by the institutions issuing them
- usual term is one to five years

CDIC DEPOSIT INSURANCE

The Canada Deposit Insurance Corporation (CDIC) is a federal government agency that insures eligible deposits at member institutions. These include most banks and trust companies in Canada, but check if you're not sure whether a particular institution qualifies. If it does, your eligible deposits are automatically insured. "Eligible" means, generally, savings, GICs, chequing, and term deposits in Canadian dollars. GICs must be repayable within five years. The maximum amount the CDIC will protect in one name at one institution is $60,000 in principal and interest in all your deposits and accounts. If you have more to invest, spread it around among two or more institutions, depositing no more than $60,000 in each (allowing for interest). Using more than one branch of the same institution will not increase your coverage. However, there are other ways to increase your coverage: eligible joint deposits and RRSP or RRIF deposits are insured separately. Each name or group of names is entitled to as much as $60,000 coverage for eligible deposits. Investments not eligible include debentures, foreign currency accounts, stocks, mutual funds, mortgages, treasury bills, and most bonds.

Government bonds

- these bonds are a way of lending the government money for a fixed interest rate
- interest income is fully taxable each year when held outside of an RRSP
- a safe and easy investment
- available at most financial institutions
- set at a fixed interest rate
- can be traded, resulting in a taxable capital gain or loss

Corporate bonds

- these bonds are issued by a company and are a way of lending that company a fixed sum of money for a fixed amount of time at a fixed interest rate
- interest income is fully taxable each year when held outside of an RRSP
- can be safe or risky, depending on the company issuing the bond
- usually purchased through stock brokers
- usually easy to cash
- can be traded, resulting in a taxable capital gain or loss

Mortgages

- this type of investment lends money to a person or a pool of people to finance their homes, and is secured by the value of the property
- interest income is fully taxable each year when held outside of an RRSP
- safe or risky depending on the borrower
- have fixed or variable interest rates
- can be difficult to sell; however, a sale could trigger a taxable capital gain or loss

Strip bonds

(also called separately traded residual and interest payments, strip coupons, zero coupons, and term investment growth receipts)

- safer if government bonds rather than corporate bonds are involved
- bought at a "discounted" price, it yields the full amount at maturity
- deemed interest income is fully taxable each year when held outside of an RRSP (This is a complex topic — contact a financial advisor for more information.)
- redeemable for a set amount at a future date (up to 30 years later)
- can be traded, resulting in a taxable capital gain or loss

Types of Equities

Common and preferred shares

Equity investments are more volatile than fixed income investments because the demand and supply for shares that determines their market value can be influenced by a number of factors. Share prices rise and fall with a company's earnings and prospects, and the health of the market, in general. Many factors are involved: rumours, government regulations, competition, and other developments that are impossible to predict. You hope to profit by selling the shares for more than you paid for them, creating a capital gain. You may also receive dividends — regular payments in cash or shares that give shareholders a piece of the company's profits. If the company has issued preferred shares, they may carry the bulk of the dividend, leaving little or none for common shareholders. The latter, however, get most of the benefit if the company's value rises.

Equities range from quite stable to wildly speculative, but even the safest can be more volatile than most fixed-income instruments. They can be very rewarding (in the long term, equities usually bring the greatest returns), but they can also make you

Shares: (also called **stocks**) A share is a portion of the ownership of a company.

Bonds: A bond is a certificate that proves that you have lent a sum of money to a company or a government for a set amount of time at a fixed interest rate.

Common shares: Owning common shares in a company means that you actually own a part of that company. If the company's value on the stock market increases, you will make a profit; if it decreases, you will experience a loss.

Preferred shares: These shares pay a fixed dividend. If the company that issued the shares does poorly, the preferred shareholders are guaranteed to receive the dividend before common shareholders get anything. (If the company does *really* poorly, no one gets anything!) Conversely, if the company does really well, the preferred shareholder gets only the fixed dividend, and usually doesn't share in any "windfall" dividends.

Mutual funds: A mutual fund pools money from thousands of investors. The portfolio manager purchases a diverse portfolio of securities (stocks, bonds, and money market instruments, etc.) on behalf of the fund investors according to the fund's objectives. Diversification typically makes this kind of investment less risky than buying individual stocks.

nervous. At the nail-biting end are the penny stocks that rise and fall fast enough to take your breath away — and your money, too.

Remember that the more aggressively you play the stock market, the more hazardous it can be to your investments (and your sleep), especially in the short term. You should keep a cash cushion for emergencies. You need to know what you are doing. If you don't have time to manage your investments, find a financial advisor you trust who can help you build the right mix of investments. If you want to start investing but have little saved or don't have the knowledge to keep up to date, you're probably better off starting with a mutual fund.

Mutual Funds

Everyone knows about mutual funds, but not necessarily how they work. A fund pools money from thousands of investors to invest in a portfolio of securities on behalf of the investors, according to the fund's objectives. The securities can include one or more of the usual categories: stocks, bonds, real estate, money market instruments, or other investments.

This has several advantages. Diversification generally lowers your risk, but it's difficult to buy a variety of things if you don't have much money to invest. However, you can buy units in a mutual fund for as little as $500, and presto — it's diversified. The investment choices are made by full-time professional management teams with years of experience and expertise, who can thoroughly assess each investment in the portfolio. Fund managers often meet with the people who run the companies they invest in — something few individual investors could hope to do. Global markets can be difficult and risky for individuals; share prices of high-quality stocks may put them out of the reach of the small investor. However, mutual funds give you access to both. They're flexible, as well; you can choose a variety of funds, as your needs dictate. Finally, mutual fund investments are not locked in, so you can

MUTUAL FUND POPULARITY

Everybody's doing it — your co-workers, your next-door neighbour, and maybe even your grandchildren. But are your capital and rate of return guaranteed? No. Mutual funds are not protected by deposit insurance, such as CDIC. You are protected if the mutual fund management company goes under, since mutual fund assets are held in trust. The fund trustee would hire a new manager to administer the assets. But remember, there are no performance guarantees. If the value of the fund's holdings drops, the value of your investment drops.

SERVICE CHARGES AND FEES

1) Management Fees
  - based on the value and growth of the fund
  - about 0.5 to 3 percent of the asset value of the fund for the management and administration of the fund

2) No-load Funds
  - units sold without any sales charge or commission fee; watch for higher management fees or hidden costs

3) Front-end Load Funds
  - charge a percentage of your total investment at the time of investment, meaning that not all of the money you invest goes into the mutual fund. Generally not more than 5 percent

4) Rear/Back-end Load Funds
  - commission is deducted when you redeem your investment — the longer you hold a mutual fund, the lower the redemption fee is. After a designated period, the back-end load usually disappears.

generally redeem them at any time. The fund manager tracks all your transactions and provides regular statements and the information you need to file your annual income taxes. Of course, all those advantages come at a price. Managers charge a management fee to the fund for their services. In addition, you might pay a "load," or sales commission, to get into or out of many funds.

There are all sorts of mutual funds, offering very diverse investments. Here are a few of the common types.

Money market funds

- aim to provide income, liquidity, and safety of capital through investment in short-term money market vehicles (treasury bills, commercial paper of companies and government, etc.)
- return earned from interest paid on the investments
- low risk

Mortgage funds
- invest in residential and commercial mortgages
- achieve most return from income earned on mortgages and potential return from capital gains
- low risk in the case of residential mortgage funds, mortgage-backed securities, and commercial mortgages

Bond or income funds
- invest in the bonds of governments and privately held or publicly traded corporations
- return results from the interest income on bonds held and on potential capital gains
- low to medium risk, depending on type of issuing companies, governments, interest rate, economic environment, etc.

Dividend funds
- provide tax-advantaged dividend income with some possibility of capital growth
- invest in preferred and common shares
- medium risk

Balanced funds
- aim for some safety of principal and a balance between income and capital appreciation
- invest in a mix of stocks and bonds
- return realized from income earned from investments, as well as from capital gains
- medium risk

Equity funds
- medium to high risk, depending on type of stock
- aim to provide capital gains or appreciation
- invest in common shares
- prices can fluctuate in value more widely than other mutual funds

- return is the result of capital gains and income from its dividends

International and global funds

- medium to high risk, depending on objectives of the fund, currency fluctuations, geographic area, etc.
- seek opportunities in international markets that offer the best prospects for growth
- invest in one or more of bonds, equities, and money market assets

Sector (industry) funds

- seek capital gains and above-average returns
- invest in a particular sector or industry
- return results from growth in value of investments
- high risk — vulnerable to swings in the particular industry

Real estate funds

- seek long-term growth through capital appreciation and the reinvestment of income
- are less liquid than other types of funds
- may require investors to give advance notice of redemption
- subject to regular valuation, based on professional appraisals of the properties in the portfolio
- high risk in recent years as a result of the real estate market

THE IMPORTANCE OF THE PROSPECTUS

A prospectus, in the investment world, is a document required by securities regulators for an offering of stock or other securities to the public. They're not easy reading, but they do contain important information about the issuer of the stock. For new companies, you should consult a professional advisor. Mutual fund companies also issue a prospectus, which states the fund's investment objectives, among other important details.

Ethical funds

- consider the ethical implications of each investment (e.g., might not invest in companies that profit from alcohol, pornography, tobacco, or armaments or in companies not meeting environmental screens)
- medium to high risk

Labour-sponsored funds

- not mutual funds but venture capital funds which must be invested in small business
- offer tax breaks to investors: the amount is different in each province
- may not be redeemable in the first five to seven years, or may face early redemption penalties, depending on provincial legislation
- redemption charges usually apply for a certain period
- high risk, liquidity poor
- governed by provincial legislation; the regulations are different in each province

Index funds

- medium to high risk
- aim is to provide capital gains
- invest in the shares of companies that are included in a particular stock market index in the same proportion [i.e., a Canadian index fund would invest in the companies that make up the Toronto Stock Exchange (TSE) 300 Composite Index; an American Index Fund would invest in the stocks that make up the Dow Jones Industrial Average]
- return is the result of capital gains and income from dividends
- managed so that it always mirrors the exchange index

Summary

Investing in a diversified portfolio is a great way to preserve assets for a comfortable retirement, but don't forget that even the safest investments carry some risk. You should take advantage of more than one of the many investment vehicles available to you. And remember that investing is an active process: you have to play a part in understanding the various types of investments. Find a financial advisor who can help you build and maintain the right mix of investments over the long term.

QUICK RECAP

1. All investments carry some risk.
2. Review what kinds of investments are suitable for you and your situation.
3. Monitor your investments.

CHAPTER 9

Disability/Incapacity

When Laszlo, the retired sales manager, was building the new back porch for his house, he fell through the boards and twisted an ankle. Laszlo and Sally were both relieved that it was only a minor accident, but it made them think about what would have happened if the accident had been worse. Sally remembered that it had been years since they had updated their wills, and Laszlo realized that he had no idea how much money Sally had made in her importing business, or how Sally wanted it invested if she was unable to do the investing herself. The whole topic of disability and incapacity makes Laszlo queasy, but Sally convinced him that after 35 years of marriage, they should finally take a serious look at this topic, for each other, their children, and their grandchildren.

Sharing Responsibilities

If you're married and one or the other of you did most of the money managing, retirement is a good time to start sharing that responsibility. This way, both of you will have control over your future and both will have the knowledge to deal with finances if the other becomes ill. If you don't plan for this possibility, the healthier spouse will be left alone to cope with this job at an already stressful time.

Disability As a Senior and Your Canada/Quebec Pension Plan

If you become disabled as a senior, you may be able to apply to have your retirement pension replaced by a CPP/QPP disability pension. According to CPP/QPP legislation, you will only be eligible to do this if you become disabled before you're 65, and if your disability started no later than six months after your retirement pension began. Whether or not this helps your finances will depend on many factors. Generally, the monthly disability benefit maximums are higher than the maximum amounts you're entitled to receive in a retirement pension. Talk to your federal income security representative (look up "income security" in the government pages of your phone book) to learn more about your eligibility and to get an estimate of any amounts you'd be entitled to receive.

Power of Attorney

If you ever become incapable of managing your own affairs, you will need someone to look after your finances. This is the person to whom you grant power of attorney. If you don't appoint someone, your loved ones will have to apply to the courts to be given the power to manage your affairs. If they do not do this, the public trustee's office will administer your affairs.

The person you appoint has the power to act on your behalf in all financial affairs, and to sign your legal documents. That person should be trustworthy, competent, objective, and familiar with your financial affairs, so for most people, a spouse is the ideal candidate. Other choices might include an adult child, your lawyer, or a trust company.

It's a good idea to grant an enduring power of attorney. This will allow the person you appoint to act on your behalf if you become mentally incompetent. An enduring power of attorney remains in effect until you die (unless you terminate it). At that time, control of your estate passes to the executor of your will.

A power of attorney can also be "general" or "restricted." With a general power of attorney, all your assets are covered. With a restricted power of attorney, you set out the specific conditions you want met.

Power of attorney for personal care

A power of attorney for personal care is available in some provinces. It gives the person of your choice the power to make decisions about your personal care (health care, nutrition, clothing, hygiene, and safety) if you become incapable of caring for yourself. The attorney for personal care is obliged to make personal care decisions in accordance with your wishes. The power of attorney for personal care can authorize someone to give or refuse consent to certain kinds of treatment for you, under specified circumstances. These specifications could be in the power of attorney document or in a living will. See your lawyer to find out the rules for your province and for assistance in drafting a power of attorney for personal care.

Living Will

A living will is a document that expresses your desire to not receive life support treatment that may artificially sustain or prolong your life. Several provinces have taken initiatives to legislate individuals' rights to determine their own health care. A living will, or health care directive, allows you to express your wishes regarding your care and treatment in situations where you are unable to communicate. The legislation usually allows for the appointment of a proxy who will act on your behalf in giving instructions for medical treatment; this is important because your directive may not address treatment in all your potential care situations. Your lawyer can tell you the rules for your province and help you draft a living will.

Long Term Care

Long term care can be very expensive both for you and the government. Many seniors are therefore trying to remain independent longer than ever. Many home care programs are now available. These, too, are usually partially funded by the province after the senior is assessed and care needs have been established.

You may find temporary relief from home care at an adult day care or through respite programs in your community. Assistance can be as simple as having your meals made and delivered to you through an organization such as Meals on Wheels. Speak to your provincial seniors' program representative for details on who pays for what.

Once a person is deemed eligible for nursing home care by a doctor, that person will be admitted to a facility. There are three types of nursing home/retirement home facilities: privately owned homes, homes built with government funding, and homes built by charitable organizations. Regardless of the type of home, the province will pay a percentage of the cost, and the resident or family will pay the balance. The cost to the family will depend on the level of care and the range of services offered. If you opt for a nursing home, don't forget to ask these questions:

- What are the terms and fees? (Nursing homes generally charge a daily or monthly rate.)
- What is and isn't included in those fees? Are laundry and physical therapy extra?
- Will costs increase if your condition deteriorates?
- What factors are taken into account by the province to determine how much of the cost the family will pay?

Life Insurance

Do you still need life insurance?

As you age, your life insurance needs change a lot. Most life insurance is sold to protect against the risk of early death and the fear that survivors won't be able to make ends meet without your income. However, if you made insurance arrangements years ago, the children you wanted to provide for may now be self-sufficient. You may wish to surrender your policy and invest the cash value, after tax, to generate supplemental retirement income.

You may, for different reasons, want to increase your life insurance protection as you age. If you have accumulated a large estate, you may want life insurance to pay the estate liabilities, such as tax on capital gains. Or, if your estate is small, perhaps you want to leave your life insurance as a cash inheritance. If you started your family or a second family later in life, maybe you have minor dependants to think about, or an adult child who is still dependent on you for support.

Evaluating existing policies

You may have a whole life policy, which you bought 35 years ago, that has accumulated a cash value you could be using now.

Or the universal life policy you bought in the early 1980s hasn't lived up to its potential annual yield. Or you've just realized your employment group life insurance ended when you retired and you were counting on it in your overall insurance strategy.

You have a whole variety of options. You can replace one insurance policy with another, "cash in" a cash value policy in return for a steady income, or lend yourself money from a cash value policy. You're also free to change beneficiary designations, transfer ownership of a policy, or convert a cash value policy to reduced, paid up insurance. However, if you "cash in" a policy, or transfer the ownership of the policy, a portion of the cash value may become taxable income. Ask your insurer to calculate the taxable benefit, if there is any, before you take action.

New policies

Because the price of life insurance is based on the risk of dying, prices increase with age and health status. People are generally living longer; therefore, rates for life insurance have been falling. However, it's still true that the older you get, the more you pay for a new life insurance policy.

Some companies have developed products for people over 50 and decide whether or not to accept the risk of insuring clients on the basis of a number of factors, in addition to age and sex. They look at things like a client's health history, occupation, hobbies, and lifestyle. So, if your overall risk is lower because these other factors weigh in your favour, you may still be able to get life insurance at a reasonable cost.

To decide which options best suit your situation, be sure you have all the information on your existing policies. Then, seek the advice of a financial planning professional who has a proven track record in handling products for seniors.

Summary

You never know when you might become disabled and lose the ability to take care of yourself, your spouse, and family finances. Although no one wants to think about this kind of tragedy, it's very common that one spouse has to make important decisions for the other at some point in their lives. Take some time to plan how you want your affairs managed if you are in a state where you cannot manage them yourself, and have your spouse do the same. This will take undue pressure off of you and your family in the long run.

QUICK RECAP

1. If your spouse does the finances in your family, start sharing the responsibility, in case you ever have to take over.

2. Have your lawyer prepare a power of attorney (and a living will) to provide for your care if you become incapacitated.

3. Evaluate your insurance policies every three to five years, more often if there are major changes in your life.

CHAPTER 10

Life's First Certainty: Taxes

It's Legal!

Now that we've talked a little bit about how to invest your money, let's talk about how to reduce or defer some of the taxes payable on your investments, so that you can continue to live the good life.

Personal Income Tax

Make up for any lost time by checking out the ways you can reduce your income taxes now. This is especially important if you or your spouse has moved into a different tax bracket since the last time you did your taxes. A financial advisor can tell you exactly what you are eligible for. By working together, you can find ways to get the most out of tax deductions and credits. Following are a few benefits you might be interested in:

- **Spousal credit**: Depending on the income of your spouse, you may be eligible for a tax credit.
- **Disability credit**: You can also receive a disability credit for supporting your spouse if he or she doesn't need to claim it.
- **Medical expense credits**: This credit is based on total expenses exceeding 3 percent of your net income, so it makes sense for the spouse who earns less to claim all of the medical expenses for your family.
- **Infirm dependants over 18**: If you have an infirm child who is over 18 years old, you can receive a credit for the cost of the care of your child.
- **Equivalent-to-spouse exemption**: This exemption can be claimed by singles, so ask a financial advisor if you are single and have any relative living with you who depends on your income.
- **Charitable donations credit**: Whenever you donate to a registered charity — to your alma mater, international aid organizations, or medical research societies — remember to keep the receipt for your income tax return.
- **Investment counsel or management fees deduction**: The fees that you pay for professional financial counselling services are tax-deductible — yet another reason to use a financial advisor!

Taxing Investments

One of the predictable ironies of investing is that the better you do, the better the government does. Every gain you make through your investment dollar is taxed by the government, but different kinds of investment gains are taxed differently. Here's how it breaks down:

Interest

Interest income — for example, money you earn on debt instruments such as bonds and GICs — is fully taxed. That is, if your marginal tax rate (your "tax bracket") is 50 percent, and you earn $1,000 in interest, then you'll pay the government $500 of that in tax.

Dividends

Dividends from Canadian companies are taxed differently than income from other sources. A dividend is an amount paid by a corporation to shareholders as a form of profit-sharing, and since the corporation has already paid tax on that income, the government has devised a tax credit system to reduce double taxation. The dividend received is increased by 25 percent, but there is a combined federal and provincial tax credit of approximately 20 percent of the grossed-up dividend of a Canadian corporation. For example, consider what happens when someone in the 50 percent tax bracket gets a $1,000 dividend. The dividend is grossed up to $1,250, so the tax is 50 percent of that, or $625. But there is also a tax credit of $250, so the total tax paid is $625 minus $250, or $375.

Capital gains

A capital gain (or loss) is the difference between the buying price and the selling price of an investment. If you make a capital gain on an investment, three quarters (75 percent) of the gain is taxable and it is taxed at your marginal tax rate. A capital loss can offset a capital gain, so get advice on timing if you are selling investments.

Tax Shelters

Of course, the most popular and often used tax shelter is the RRSP. And, so long as you have "earned income" from wages, salaries, net rental income, and royalties you can continue to contribute to your RRSP until the end of the year you turn 69. After 69, you can still contribute to a spousal RRSP until the end of the year in which your spouse turns 69 if you have earned income. Your contribution limits, as always, will be based on your previous year's earnings plus unused contribution room carried forward.

Other types of tax shelters

There are other, more exotic types of tax shelters, such as tax credits related to the film industry, that you are bound to hear about. Be cautious with these shelters and don't get involved unless you have received thorough professional advice.

Summary

We all have to pay taxes, but the amount you pay can be drastically reduced with some smart planning, such as using all of your tax credits. These aren't illegal loopholes and you're not cheating the tax system, you're taking advantage of programs that the government set up for you to use. As well, don't forget that you pay tax on your total income, including the income you receive from your investments. Different investments are taxed at different rates, so bear this in mind when doing your tax planning. Be sure to talk to a financial advisor about the tax implication of any major life event (such as a retirement, death, marriage, or divorce).

QUICK RECAP

1. Make sure you and your spouse take advantage of the tax credits for common-law or married couples.

2. Your investments are taxable — be sure you know what rate of tax you pay on which investments.

3. A financial advisor can guide you to tax breaks you may not find on your own.

CHAPTER 11

Life's Last Certainty: Death

Estate Planning

Maybe you think that death is the last thing you need to worry about, since once you're gone, it's not your problem, is it? But it will be your family's problem. By creating a solid estate plan, you will ensure that the people you care about are looked after when you're gone. You'll also have peace of mind in knowing that your affairs will be looked after in accordance with your wishes. Estate planning ensures that what you leave behind goes where you want it. If it's done right, you'll be able to transfer and preserve your wealth in an effective and orderly manner. It also helps minimize taxation, probate fees, delays, and family conflict on death.

Your Estate

Estate planning is the best way to ensure that your wishes for the disposition of your assets upon your death are carried out and that your assets will be passed on in a timely and tax effective way. This is true whether you have a large estate or only modest assets. With proper planning, you can maximize the benefits to your heirs and keep as much of your money as possible out of the government's pockets.

There are many ways you can pass on assets to your beneficiaries, either before or after your death.

- Giving gifts during your lifetime
- Setting up trusts during your lifetime
- Establishing joint ownership of assets
- Designating beneficiaries
- Estate freezing
- Preparing a will

Gifts by will can be by bequest to beneficiaries or be held under the terms of a trust for a beneficiary. Most transfers of assets trigger tax consequences, so you should consult a professional advisor when planning your estate and considering these types of giving.

Gifts During Your Lifetime

People who want to retain control over their assets may choose not to give gifts during their lifetime. However, there may be advantages to gifting a particular asset to a beneficiary during your lifetime. For instance, if you give a gift while you are alive, you avoid the probate and other fees on its value upon your death. As well, legal fees are often based on the total value of your estate. You are no longer taxable on income and capital gains earned on the asset after you transfer ownership (providing you are not giving it to your spouse, a minor child, a grandchild, or someone else to whom the "attri-bution rules" apply.)

Before you make the gift, consider the potential drawbacks. You will trigger a capital gain when you transfer a capital asset that is worth more than you paid for it. This would require you to pay tax on any capital gain (in the case of a transfer of cap-ital asset to your spouse, the property can be transferred at adjusted cost base). If you gift an asset to your spouse or to a minor child, income (and capital gains, in the case of a spouse) will be attributed back to you on the original gift. Keep in mind that you will lose control of the asset once the gift is made. There are many issues to consider before gifting assets — be sure that you speak to your professional advisor first.

Setting Up Trusts During Your Lifetime (Inter Vivos Trusts)

Trusts are a way of ensuring your wishes for use of your assets are acted upon, both while you are alive and after you die. That is, it is a way to impose conditions on the beneficiary's access to and use of your assets. As the "settlor," you transfer your property into the trust, which is managed by a "trustee" who sees that the trust property is managed for the benefit of your "beneficiaries" in accordance with the terms and conditions of the trust. There are many ways to use trusts, to provide for both minor and adult beneficiaries.

Trusts allow you to transfer beneficial ownership of an asset to an individual or a charity while you establish conditions on the beneficiary's access to the asset. An inter vivos trust is one that is established to take effect while you are alive. Some rea-sons to consider an inter vivos trust are as follows:

1. It can offer long-term income and protection for minor children or dependants who are not able to look after themselves or handle their own financial matters.

2. It can be part of an "estate freeze" (see below) structure where your asset value is frozen and future asset growth is transferred to the next generation.

3. It can provide lifetime income from an asset to one beneficiary and preserve the capital for the benefit of another on the death of the first. It can impose conditions on a beneficiary's use of an asset.

4. It can create a trust for charitable purposes.

5. It can be a discreet way of giving, apart from your will, which becomes public when probated.

6. It can protect family assets.

7. It can achieve income splitting with an adult family member who has a lower marginal tax rate.

Joint Ownership and Designation of Beneficiaries

You can minimize your probate fees by removing assets from your estate, but there are certain risks to doing so. Be sure to consult a professional advisor first! There are two ways to do this: register property or bank accounts jointly so that they automatically pass through to the survivor, although this means sharing ownership and control of the asset during your lifetime. Designate beneficiaries to your insurance, RRSPs, and RRIFs. **Caution:** there can be tax and other consequences associated with adding an individual as a joint owner of capital property, as well as designating that individual as beneficiary.

Estate Freezing

An estate freeze is a procedure that may be used if you currently own an asset but wish to have any future increase in the value of the asset be taxed in the hands of someone else — usually family members — thereby locking-in, or "freezing," the value of your interest. This strategy serves to limit your tax liability on growth by having the growth accrue to the new owners after the date of the estate freeze. This is a complex procedure that requires professional tax advice.

Do You Need a Will?

Everyone needs a will. The first and biggest risk of dying without a will is that your property won't be distributed as you wish! Also, the delays in getting your estate distributed may be longer than otherwise, as the court needs to appoint someone to act as your administrator. That person will likely have to post a bond, which is an additional expense.

Having a will allows you to appoint a trusted person or trust company as executor and to save your survivors time, money, and stress. It also allows you to effectively plan the distribution of your estate to pay the lowest amount of estate and income taxes possible.

What Happens If You Die without a Will?

Just like the probate fees, the intestate succession laws vary between provinces. Generally, your estate is split between your spouse and children (if you have both), in one way or another. It could be that your spouse will receive one third and your children will split the other two thirds equally, or that your spouse receives half and your children split the other half. In all provinces, if you only have a spouse or only have children, the entire estate goes to them.

Drafting Your Will

A will is a legal document that sets out how you want your assets to be disposed of and distributed. It can be rewritten or amended at any time and only comes into effect after you die. Your will also names an executor, the person or corporation (in cases where a trust company acts as the executor) who will deal with your property.

It's a good idea to hire a lawyer to draw up your will. You can do it yourself, but unless you comply with all the formalities, your will could end up invalid. A will that you draw up by yourself could also be subject to misinterpretation, fail to deal with all of your property, neglect to take advantage of tax elections, or have other flaws that turn out to be very expensive.

Your will includes:

- the name of your executor and a description of his or her powers;
- a list of beneficiaries and specific bequests and legacies; and
- terms of any trusts to be established.

Reviewing your will at least every three to five years, and at important events in your life (marriage, divorce, death of a family member), will keep it up-to-date with changes in your life.

Naming an executor

You may want to name a family member or friend as executor because you trust them or because you know they are familiar with your finances. In most cases, this is great, but it is not always the ideal situation. A family member or friend will already be under a great deal of stress at the time of your death. He or she may also not have the knowledge and time necessary to do the job well. Many people consider their lawyer to be a good choice. But unless your lawyer has experience in estate administration, this could be a mistake. Another option is to appoint a trust company as executor if your situation is complicated or if you simply want to spare your loved ones the work. A trust company has the facilities, experience, and time to handle the valuations, paperwork, and other duties of managing your affairs, but be aware of the company's fees for this service.

If your estate is fairly straightforward and your spouse or adult child knows the details of your finances, he or she might be the best choice. If you feel strongly about keeping your spouse involved but worry about how complicated and time-consuming it will be, consider naming an experienced and knowledgeable co-executor. They can then work together in handling your estate efficiently and according to your wishes. It's also important that in your will, you give your executor(s) enough power to make appropriate investment and taxation decisions for you.

Whomever you appoint as executor, a fee can be payable for the work they do. Most provinces set a limit of 5 percent of the probatable assets, which applies whether your executor is a lawyer, an individual, or a trust company.

Spousal Rollover of Property

The Income Tax Act allows for a transfer of capital property to your legal or common-law spouse, on a tax deferred basis, at the adjusted cost base rather than at fair market value. Remember that the spousal attribution rules will continue to apply until you, as the transferror, die or become a non-resident. Capital gains and simple income from the investments will attribute back to you even though you have transferred the property to your spouse.

Spousal Rollover of RRSPs and RRIFs

Upon your death, under certain conditions, RRSPs, RRIFs, or registered annuities can be rolled over to the registered plan of a surviving spouse without triggering any immediate tax liability. This has to be done carefully, so be sure to consult your professional advisor. Otherwise, your estate will be responsible for the taxes on the value of the plan as of the date of death.

Setting Up a Testamentary Trust

Trusts are one way of dealing with your assets after you die. They come with income-tax opportunities and burdens, depending on your circumstances. You need a lawyer to help

HELPFUL HINT

To protect minors, your will can establish a trust for their legacies. If you're concerned about the free-spending habits of your heirs, you can set out a plan for paying their inheritance in instalments.

you with this. Your property is transferred into the testamentary trust on your death. It is managed by a "trustee," who is responsible for carrying out the terms of the trust. There are many ways to use trusts, to provide for both minor and adult heirs.

Select a trustee

To create a trust to take effect upon your death, the trust is included as a provision of your will. There are two kinds of trustees: corporate trustees, such as a trust company; or individual trustees, such as a family member, lawyer, or friend. The position of trustee comes with a lot of responsibility. Appointing a family member is one possibility. A corporate trustee is also an option.

Spousal trust

An example of a testamentary trust is one that can be established to provide your spouse with income for life, but leave the capital for other beneficiaries such as children or grandchildren. This has the advantage of ensuring that the children or grandchildren ultimately get the capital property.

Minimizing the Cost of Dying

What we commonly refer to as estate taxes usually includes costs such as probate and legal fees when a will is validated, and income taxes that become due upon death.

In the year of death, you are deemed by the Income Tax Act to have disposed of all capital property immediately before your death at fair market value. Three quarters of the taxable capital gains are taxed in the hands of your estate. So, even though your property has not actually been sold, tax is still payable on it as though it had been sold just prior to your death. Also, the value of your RRSP/RRIF will be taxed on your final return unless they are rolled to an RRSP/RRIF for your spouse.

Probate Fees

Probate fees vary widely from province to province and change frequently. Most provinces charge a percentage of the value of the estate. Some provinces have a flat probate fee (for example, $10 on every $1,000, or portion thereof). Check the current fees in your province.

Deceased's Tax Returns

Special income tax rules apply to the filing of returns for deceased persons, and a number of elections are available, which could mean considerable tax savings. It's important that your executor — the person responsible for filing these returns — obtain the information necessary to take advantage of these rules.

Planned Giving to a Charity

Many people feel a certain loyalty to a given charitable cause and want to show their loyalty through giving. Before you do this, you should first be sure that your favourite charity is registered with Revenue Canada and is able to issue receipts that qualify for the charitable tax credit. By planning your charitable gifts you may be able to increase the tax benefit of your donation, leaving more money for your estate, or increasing the money you donate.

Bequests are deductible in the year of death but if the total donation exceeds the income of the current and prior year you will not receive the full tax credit. Planning to give more during your lifetime may increase the tax credits.

Gifts of publicly traded securities with an accrued capital gain will result in a better overall tax position than gifting the same amount in cash.

In a nutshell, you have many options on how to give to a charitable cause. You can give an outright gift now or make a bequest under your will. With an insurance policy, you can make your estate the beneficiary, and include the charitable bequest in your will. You can give a charitable gift annuity or set up a charitable remainder trust or a private charitable foundation. When making your choice, you should consider some of the following factors:

1. Is the gift subject to probate and executor fees?
2. When is the charitable tax credit available: annually or at the time of death?
3. Is there a minimum amount required for this to qualify as a charitable donation?
4. Can you revoke the gift?
5. Do you get the income from or use of the gift during your lifetime?
6. When can the charity use the gift?
7. Can you specify how the charity should use the gift?

Whatever your choice, with proper planning, tax savings can fund up to 40 percent of your gift. It's therefore very important that you get appropriate advice before deciding exactly how to go about it.

Make an Estate Plan

Without an estate plan, you won't even know what will be left over for your beneficiaries. Following are the basic elements that your plan should have:

1. Determine the value of your estate. Look at the net worth statement you prepared in Chapter 2. Your assets should include any lump-sum benefits from your company pension plan, CPP/QPP, and life insurance.

2. Anticipate your estate's liabilities:
   - **Funeral costs** (you can prepay them by putting the money in a trust where it can earn some interest)
   - **Executor or administrator fee** (3 to 5 percent of the estate value)
   - **Legal fees** (should be less than 2 percent of the estate value)
   - **Probate fees** (court fees vary from province to province, but are based on the value of the estate)
   - **Trustee fees**
   - **Taxes** (capital gains taxes don't apply to assets that are transferred to your surviving spouse, but everything else is deemed to be sold at the date of death; three quarters of the capital gain is taxable on your final tax return; the principal-residence exemption still applies and special roll-overs are available for certain farm property and some shares of Canadian-controlled private corporations)

3. Subtract your costs from the value of your estate to determine what you will be leaving to your beneficiaries.

Summary

Death is not a very popular subject, but you and your family will benefit financially and emotionally from getting this matter in order. The best way to afford more time for healing and less time for legal and financial confusion should you or your spouse die, is to each draft a legally binding will. This will provide you, your spouse, and your dependants knowledge that they will be well taken care of after your death, and that everything you worked so hard for will go where you want it to. This may seem like a grim business, but estate planning is an integral part of financial planning, and the sooner you do it, the better you will feel about your future and that of your dependants.

QUICK RECAP

1. All investments are taxed differently: make sure you know how much tax you will be paying on yours.

2. If you don't already have a will, get one now!

3. To avoid as many problems as possible for your family, determine how your estate will be dealt with after your death.

CHAPTER 12

Ready, Set, Go!

Get Ready to Enjoy the Rest of Your Life

Now that you've read this far, you know that planning to use your retirement finances wisely isn't half as intimidating as you once thought. Just like Lloyd, Sally, and Laszlo, you have learned about the different retirement options available to you, and know if you are making the best choices to meet your needs and desires. As you can see, your dreams can be realized. Congratulations! This knowledge puts you far ahead of many people who are too afraid to begin even thinking about how their finances have changed since they retired, let alone take charge of them.

Until this stage in your life, you may have gotten by without putting much planning into how to keep your household running. But that was when you were earning an income, before you started living on a fixed retirement income. Now, managing your cash flow can make the difference between just getting by and retiring comfortably, with the freedom to do what you want for the rest of your life.

That doesn't mean that you have to guard against spending any of your nest egg. It just means taking stock of where you are and where you want to go. Then you can make the smart decisions to get you there. Managing your retirement income should become part of your life, just don't let it take over your life.

The whole point of financial health is to follow a few sensible steps to become financially secure enough to live the way you want to. It's up to you how you invest and spend your money.

ONE MORE TIME

As we told you in Chapter 1, the key to sound financial management and a secure financial future is to assess your situation regularly. Here's a review:

At least once a year, assess your financial situation as well as your long-term and short-term financial goals. Establish a realistic and comfortable plan to achieve those goals. Implement your plan, keeping in mind your risk tolerance and time horizon. Use a financial advisor the same way you would use a doctor — take advantage of their expertise to ensure your financial health.

It's easy. Think of it as your annual review. Don't forget to include the following:

- net worth
- budget
- will
- retirement goals
- investment portfolio
- insurance needs

General Summary

1. Do a self-assessment, re-prioritize your goals.

2. Assess your net worth at least annually.

3. Taxes on different types of investment income vary. Get professional advice on creating a tax-effective income stream.

4. Work to eliminate debt.

5. Consider how the purchase of new assets will affect the rest of your retirement.

6. Review your risk tolerance and adjust your investment portfolio accordingly.

7. Plan ahead for the RRSP conversion date: will you want a RRIF, an annuity, or a combination of the two?

8. If retirement takes you outside of Canada, familiarize yourself with the tax laws of your destination country as well as Canada's.

9. Don't be caught by financial surprise if disability or incapacity strikes. Grant a power of attorney now and discuss your wishes with your family.

10. Review your estate plan regularly.

Then, sit back and enjoy!

Index